FRENCH ESSENCE

VICKI ARCHER

Photographs by Carla Coulson

VIKING STUDIO

For David, always for you

CONTENTS

PREVIOUS PAGES - (pages iv-v) L'Atelier Paul Cézanne, Aix-en-Provence.
(pages vi-vii) The Palais des Fapes, Avignon.
LEFT - Chinoiserie wallpaper in the Chinese Cabinet room at La Mirande, Avignon.

INTRODUCTION

THE TWO WORDS THAT WOULD BEST DESCRIBE my last ten years are chance and change. Chance led me to Saint Rémy de Provence and with that has come change. Looking back I cannot believe that a chance encounter in a foreign country could change a life in so many different ways. The publication of *My French Life* in 2006 made me aware that I am not alone in my deep love for France and that there are so many like-minded souls and kindred spirits who share my enthusiasm for all things French.

French Essence continues my love affair with France and in particular Provence, where I live. Beautiful surroundings have always fuelled my creative soul and to live life here with such an abundance of nature and loveliness is a gift. I questioned what it was that makes my life in Provence unique and what is so great the attraction – the answer was simple: ambience. Ambience is the single ingredient that distinguishes and infuses life here; *French Essence* is a written and photographic celebration of this. To explore Avignon, the City of Popes, to follow the footsteps of Cézanne in Aix-en-Provence, to watch an exquisite sunset over the Valley of Les Baux de Provence or to relax in a favourite room that flickers with candlelight is to feel a part of this ambience.

I have been a lover of architecture, art, furniture and decor forever, and French interiors – whether public or private – are full of imagination and flair. The French have opened my eyes to colour and taught me to applaud originality and be free of the traditional restraints when it comes to decorating. I am no longer afraid to mix the old with the new or the formal with the informal. I have learnt that the best interiors come from the heart and from a passion for collecting. *French Essence* is about the relationship between ambience and our surroundings; it is about finding the inspiration and the guidance outside to enhance our lives on the inside.

As a believer in fate I like to think that the path I follow is the right one for me. I never doubt its direction and I happily embrace all the left and rights along the way. The beauty of fate and accepting change is that it is impossible to predict an outcome. I never imagined I would lead a French life and nor would I have imagined a life as olive farmer, writer and blogger, but as a result of my chance encounter in Provence my life has been enriched immeasurably. I am inspired on a daily basis and I work with talented and innovative people from all over the world doing what I love most. What could be better?

Vicki Archer

AMBIENCE

I

LIKE TO THINK THAT IN FRANCE there is a sixth sense – a French sense.

There is a certain something about the French and the style in which they live that creates a unique ambience. Their success lies in the inherent ability to blend all the senses, which makes for a life that is filled with emotion and a life in which the senses are forever stimulated. Ambience permeates every aspect of French Life, whether it be in private spaces or public places.

Les spectacles – celebrations, exhibitions, festivals, concerts and theatre productions – are all conducted with panache. Watching a summer concert or opera in Provence is captivating. High up in the Roman amphitheatre of Orange I have sobbed for *Madame Butterfly* and had goose bumps in Lacoste listening to the music of Edith Piaf and Jacques Brel. Sitting draped over the balcony in Avignon's Opera House I have found myself humming to the aria from *La traviata*. I have watched enthralled as acrobats float over Le Palais des Papes, and at the circus in Perpingnan I have held my breath as a trapeze artist swings overhead.

In France ambience is more than merely an atmosphere or mood. Atmosphere suggests something witnessed, observed, an outsider looking in; ambience, or French sense, as I call it, envelops. The right ambience can calm and comfort, it can excite and inspire, cause laughter and tears, but whatever the effect, memories are born that endure and shape life. It is not about creating perfection, it is about creating sentiment.

French sense is simple – it is chemistry, a magical mix of the sights, sounds, smells, tastes and textures that make France a wondrous place to live and one of the world's most popular countries to visit. As a nation France has chemistry, as individuals the French have spark.

I have had an ongoing love affair with France, and particularly Provence, for fifteen years, but it wasn't until 1999 – when I found my own home, Mas de Bérard in Saint-Rémy-de-Provence – that I truly appreciated this balance and harmony of the senses.

Mas de Bérard is five minutes from the village of Saint-Rémy-de Provence in south-western France, thirty minutes from Avignon, forty minutes from Aix-en-Provence and fifty minutes from the second-largest city in France, Marseille. The *mas* (farmhouse) sits in the middle of 5o acres of olive groves and fruit orchards, with a magnificent view of Les Alpilles, a small, sheltered mountain range.

Buying and restoring this property has been a labour of love from the very first moment. I discovered Mas de Bérard in 1999 while on holiday in Provence with my husband, David, and our children Emily, Venetia and Paddy. The *mas* was a vision of crumbling walls and broken roof tiles, the garden a wasteland and the fields uncultivated. For many it would have appeared an impossible task, but for me the project was compelling – I was a woman in love; I could not have stopped myself even if I had wanted to. Sheer madness and inexplicable passion can change lives: within a month we managed to exchange contracts on the property, engage an architect to oversee the restoration, and organise the planting of 3ooo olive trees. Several months later we had sold our home in Sydney and moved across the world to live between London and Saint-Rémy-de-Provence.

Today, ten years later, Mas de Bérard is in harmony. The farmhouse is truly home, the gardens are well established, the fruit trees are blooming and the olive trees are flourishing. I have become an olive farmer. The olive trees planted in 2000 are maturing and producing fruit under the watchful eye of our manager, Gérard. We work together closely and share a keen interest in the progress of the olive trees and the November harvest.

There is a sense of great peace and calm at Mas de Bérard. Our home and farm have developed their own ambience. Over the past ten years I have grown accustomed to living in a country where the senses are heightened and celebrated. The French intuitively know how to combine these elements, how to enjoy their daily lives enveloped in this ambience. Living in France I am both witness to and participant in this French sense.

I find nothing more gratifying than providing an inviting and peaceful home environment for my family and friends. I have always been fascinated by interiors – other people's homes, film and theatre sets, decorating books and magazines. I happily study, analyse and dissect as many room images as I can in order to learn more about the placement of furniture, art and objects. I believe that styling provides the backbone of perfecting ambience and it is ambience that makes a room memorable. Even the most beautiful, lavish rooms can feel lifeless without it.

Ambience must feel effortless; for those of us not born with a natural French sense, this process takes time, inspiration, observation and patience. When David is due back from a business trip, my children are coming home from university or my friends are arriving for a long weekend, I spend days fussing. It is not a chore; I can think of no better way to spend my time than on the most important people in my life. My mother did – she still does – and I hope my children will.

Ambience is about comfort. It is the feeling of silkiness after a scented-oil bath or the snuggling under a feather quilt. Comfort is the hot pounding shower at the end of the day and hair that is washed, damp and sweet-smelling. It is the soft down pillow and the cool glass of water by the bed. It is about watching a movie on a comfortable sofa, a cashmere rug over the knees, in front of the fire – the flames almost as mesmerising as the film. Comfort is feeling warm, calm and protected.

My great love – and my greatest extravagance when it comes to time spent on detail – is flowers, for their beauty and their perfume. This past spring and summer our iceberg roses have flowered prolifically, providing plenty of flowers from May until late October. As part of my weekly routine I spend time at the flower markets in Saint-Rémy-de-Provence and the neighbouring villages; each has its specialty and its own particular mood and contributes something to the interior of the *mas*.

Sometimes I decorate the *mas* not with blooms but with bowls of apples and pears from the orchard, or olive branches from the grove. It might be clipped lavender, wild rosemary and thyme or the violet sweet peas that grow along the banks of the canal that runs through our property. These floral creations add life and spirit to every room and offer a warm welcome to my family and friends.

Candles flicker in abundance at Mas de Bérard. They are a natural accessory and accomplice for the soft lighting habit that I have adopted from the French. Everyone and everything looks prettier with gentle light. I place candles everywhere around the *mas* – on the walls, on the floors, on the stairs and on the furniture. I light the scented candles every evening at dusk, and choose them depending on the season: in summer the fragrance reflects those of the garden – the fig trees, the fruit trees and the lavender beds; in winter the headier notes of cedar and cypress mix with the smoke from the wood fire. I believe that there is nothing more welcoming after a long journey than opening the door to an oasis of candlelight and fragrance.

AS WE STROLL THROUGH THE NARROW STONE STREETS of Saint-Rémy-de-Provence, the March evening is cool and the surrounds are quiet. Entering L'Ail et La Cuisse, a favourite restaurant in the village, I am struck immediately by the softness of the lighting.

LEFT - Iceberg roses arranged on a hall table at Mas de Bérard. Our Roman soldier 'dressed' for carnival.
TOP - A painted commode on the upstairs landing. A carved detail, from a mirrored panel, that hangs in the guest room.
FOLLOWING PAGE - The view across the Ancienne Voie Aurelia towards the Alpilles Mountains.

The dining room is rectangular and built of exposed limestone blocks, which are roughly hewn and irregular in shape. A chandelier is suspended by way of a massive chain in the apex of the vaulted ceiling. Each arm of this generous iron light is dressed with a red lampshade to soften the glare of the bulbs, which cast a pink wash over the room. Standard lamps with parchment shades are scattered around the room to throw light on any dark spots.

One wall of the dining room is painted with wide caramel stripes, and a chocolate-coloured velvet banquette is anchored in front. Crisp white linen cloths cover the square tables, and small ruby-red glasses hold fluttering candles and red roses; the stems of the roses are cut short and the petals are blown. The panelled wooden bar on the right-hand side of the room, opposite the banquette, is lit from a bulkhead above, encasing the glasses and bottles in subdued light. Dividing the length of the room is a tiered glass *étagère* that holds the desserts for the evening and, on the top shelf, cylindrical jars of sweets – the restaurant's signature offering with coffee and liqueur.

At the far end of the dining room sits a Provençal commode, above which hangs a portrait of a cockerel, setting the tone for more chicken memorabilia. Chickens sit on the bar, on the walls and even in the loo – that is why I refer affectionately to this place as 'the chicken restaurant'.

The music is groovy – one of those eclectic French mixes that blends a little opera, a familiar top-of-the-pops tune and some South American samba – but not too loud; we can still talk comfortably.

France is the home of taste sensation, and this is an integral key to understanding the people and their country. Life here revolves around food and wine – to dine well is a given, whomever or wherever you are.

I always order the roast *poussin* – a young chicken bred for its extra flavour and tenderness – because it is a speciality of the house and because it is seriously delicious. On each visit to L'Ail et La Cuisse I fully intend to broaden my taste horizons, but when I see *coquelet* written on the blackboard menu I remember the way this dish is served and I find myself nodding to Yvan – he doesn't need to ask for my choice, he already knows. The chicken is accompanied by morels cooked in their own jus with a touch of cream and accompanied by hand-cut oven-roasted potatoes. Sublime.

I feel relaxed and happy in this soft light, sitting in comfort and chatting with family or friends over delicious food. I feel a part of this restaurant and appreciate the fine attention to detail – the sights, the sounds, the tactile elements, the scents and the tastes that have created this ambience. L'Ail et La Cuisse truly has French sense.

N ATURE IS THE GRAND MASTER OF AMBIENCE.
The blend of colour, the clarity of light, the sounds, smells, tastes and endless textures at Mas de Bérard enchant me and are my continual source of inspiration. The smell in the air after a heavy rainfall or the touch of snowflakes on my upturned palms ... early-morning frost, the crunch of ice beneath my feet and the whirling mist . . . the luminescent green skin of the native gecko lizard and the delicate shades of a butterfly's wings . . . these can all cause my heart to stir. I love lying in bed listening as the nightingale chants to his beloved when all else is quiet. A high-pitched range of whistling, rippling shrills that reach an impressive crescendo fills our garden with such pure sound that I long to better understand the romance of music.

To watch the majestic eagles soar overhead takes my breath away and to hear the cicadas, our in-house hot weather barometer, reminds me of my Australian upbringing. When I witness the violet slashes and the vermillion streaks of the Provençal sunset, I wish I were a painter. The lessons are here to be learnt, this accord with nature is the real thing.

Ambience can make time stand still.

PREVIOUS PAGES - Newspapers stacked near the fireplace in the dining room at Mas de Bérard underneath a painting by Leonard French called 'Turtles over Temples'.
The vineyards on the Ancienne Voie Aurelia near the village of Saint Rémy de Provence.
LEFT - Candle making in the village of Graveson.

FRENCH SENSE IS SIMPLE – IT IS
CHEMISTRY, A MAGICAL MIX OF THE
SIGHTS, SOUNDS, SMELLS, TASTES
AND TEXTURES THAT MAKE FRANCE
THE MOST WONDROUS PLACE TO
LIVE AND ONE OF THE WORLD'S
MOST POPULAR COUNTRIES TO
VISIT. AS A NATION FRANCE HAS
CHEMISTRY, AS INDIVIDUALS THE
FRENCH HAVE SPARK.

COLLECTIONS

ORBIS IMPERIO VIRTUS.
virtute suâ:partas, ultimò ad Arbelam
xander, eaque, clade funditus everso
us in poteſtatem Macedonici ceſsit

I AM A COLLECTOR AND LOVER of all sorts of fanciful objects. When I see something of interest it immediately becomes grouped and categorised in my mind – where could it belong? Collections can be made up of any group of objects that are bound to each other in some way and that please the eye. One simple purchase can start a collection, or a collection can be formed by intentionally putting together like objects over time – either way it requires an enormous energy for the subject. Adding to a collection can change the direction and enhance it as a whole. A single addition can increase the value by far more than the object's individual worth – the whole is always greater than the parts. Collections can be noteworthy and of museum quality, or simple groupings of chosen objects whose value is purely sentimental.

For me the importance of the collection is far less intriguing than learning how the collection came together in the first place. Every collection tells a story, and at the same time a collection of objects is a catalogue of life.

Throughout history French collectors have been key players in the visual arts and not only actively encouraged young artists in their work but were philanthropic and patriotic in their support of museums. For previous generations, to be an active or passive collector was to engage with art in everyday life – collecting was an all-encompassing pastime and one that submerged both work and play. These collectors of the past left a legacy of taste, style and artistic inspiration that continues to live on in modern-day France.

I suspect that my soft spot for collecting springs from a genetic disposition. I grew up browsing in antique shops and specialist fairs with my mother. She was always on the lookout for furniture, vintage fabric, silver or English porcelain, and even though during my teens I found it tedious, this bent of hers for searching and collecting has rubbed off. My father was an inveterate traveller and often returned home with souvenirs of the countries he had visited; I would spend hours in my bedroom deciding the best way to display the mementos he had brought me.

I cannot remember a time in my life when I have not been looking for or arranging unusual objects. I arranged and rearranged my bedroom as a child, my first flat as a university student, and every house I have lived in during my married life. Most days I change something around at Mas de Bérard in the quest for aesthetic contentment.

In 1995 David, the children and I spent our first long stretch of time living in southern France. It was then that I started what are today some of my best-loved collections. Most weeks I would see posters on the roadside advertising an antique market in a nearby village. These outdoor markets – or *les brocantes* – ran over a Saturday and Sunday, and each weekend I would exploit my childhood training and see what treasures were on show. I was often overwhelmed by the quantity of desirable goods and I learnt early that I had to refine my search or I would come home confused and empty-handed. Today these *brocantes* are just as frequent, but both the quality and quantity of the goods have diminished and the items are more expensive. Now, ever the optimist, I try to unearth new discoveries for my collections further afield in Provence.

Rambling around these antique markets has helped me establish my own rules for collecting: I only buy what I must have and what I cannot forget; I trust my eye and follow my instinct – when I reconsider overnight I almost never return the next day, and often great opportunities are lost. I am not practical by nature and I believe that if I cannot live without an object then it cannot live without me.

I search and collect with the heart. I am an amateur in the ranks of world collectors but a professional in terms of zeal when it comes to my chosen search. A shopping list is not for the collector – a collection of objects should not be a set piece. Collecting is about taking time and knowing that the reward is not always about the acquisition but what is discovered on the journey.

I never find what I need when I purposefully look for it. I have learnt that being open-minded when searching can lead to exciting outcomes. One day several years ago David and I left the *mas* with the intention of buying a much-needed desk for his office. He had a very clear idea of what he wanted, and for more than a year we had searched village markets and antique fairs for a large but simple wooden desk with enough knee height to fit his tall frame. This particular Sunday we made a promise that our search would be confined to the desk; everything else was to be avoided.

We did not arrive home empty-handed. One broken promise later, we struggled into the *mas* with a plaster bust of a Roman soldier. He sits on an oak table in our hallway and forms an unlikely pair with another plaster compatriot. My habit is to decorate these men throughout the holiday seasons, and this eccentricity of mine has become one of our family traditions and something friends expect to see. Finding our Roman soldier has meant that I am forever on the lookout for further mates, and while our search for the desk remained elusive for a further year, a new collection was born.

A N INQUISITIVE NATURE IS AN ASSET for the collector. Talking to vendors about the provenance of their possessions can be as informative as any history lesson. I have learnt more about Provence in my quest for the fabulous find than at any other time. Struggling with the French language and displaying a natural curiosity has endeared me to the Provençals on many occasions. They are happy to open their hearts and minds to those with similar passions, and even though for some the making of a sale is never far from their thoughts, they have willingly prolonged the moment to enlighten me.

Each Tuesday, Thursday and Friday Monsieur Culat stands quietly behind his bookstall opposite the town hall in Aix-en-Provence. At our first few meetings I simply browsed, too nervous to say much, but I gradually built a rapport with Monsieur Culat, as I realised that the more eager I was to learn, the happier he was to share with me his profound knowledge. Over the past thirteen years he has shown me many splendid volumes and helped me choose the best examples for my collection. They were not his most valuable books, but that was never the point – he was intent on ensuring that I understood the differences between the various editions and that I chose only those that would enhance my collection. He remembered every volume I had bought from him and even the books I had selected for friends.

In one of our early conversations I mentioned that my favourite book is *The Count of Monte Cristo* by Alexandre Dumas and that I hankered after a French copy. He promised to look out. Over the years each visit would follow the same pattern: I would pore over his new acquisitions, listen to his marvellous stories, add to my collection and ask about *le comte*. He would shake his head wearily and apologise for the delay – he had not forgotten but 'he' was proving evasive.

As I walked through the market one glorious spring day, enjoying the lively atmosphere and appreciating the colour around me, Monsieur Culat caught my eye. A broad smile lit his face as he

LEFT – A collection of ceramic teapots.
TOP – 'The Count of Monte Christo' by Alexandre Dumas.

JANE EYRE ✤ CHARLOTTE BRONTË

beckoned to me. We barely exchanged pleasantries, such was his excitement; twelve years after I had spoken of the *The Count of Monte Cristo*, he had found my copy.

I COLLECT BECAUSE I AM REASSURED by the tangible evidence of familiar objects. I believe that the home is paramount to a contented and balanced life. Collecting is another way of creating comfort and ambience.

Our home in France showcases the life I share with my husband and children. When we moved into Mas de Bérard so did all our worldly goods from Australia. We never questioned whether they would fit or if they would work in a French context – they were part of our lives and our moving road show. Most of our art, furniture and collectibles have been chosen on our travels and hold sentimental as well as practical value.

The form a collection takes is a reflection of mood, a gauge of likes and dislikes and a chronicle of personal history. As I have aged my tastes have changed and are reflected in the objects I choose. I have sunglasses from the 1970s, shoes and bags from the 1980s and 1990s and every bit of good and bad fashion in between. These demonstrate my evolving taste and represent change through the decades.

Collections of *Architectural Digest*, *House & Garden* and *Interior* magazines from the 1960s and 1970s are timeless and continue to inspire me. *Paris Match* magazine from the late 1930s until the end of the 1940s is an illustrated record of a country at war and my current collectible.

The word 'collector' in this sense is a broad term and could be mistaken for 'hoarder', but that is a matter of opinion – I believe that what is throwaway for some is precious to others. The French *brocante* is living proof of that sentiment and a paradise for the human bowerbird.

THE TOWN OF CARPENTRAS in the region of Vaucluse is the gateway to the magical limestone-capped Mont Ventoux and about an hour's drive from Saint-Rémy-de-Provence. A regular Sunday flea market in the plane-tree-lined drive, Jean Jaures, attracts an eclectic crowd from all over Provence. The daily fruit, vegetable and flower morning market turns into a bargain bazaar of old collectibles in the afternoon. Cars, trucks and vans park alongside each other on the asphalt to create impromptu viewing avenues. The area in front of each vehicle is arranged with great care and precision to display each vendor's collection. When the dealers source their goods they are influenced by the same factors as buyers, so each piece of turf is personal. Although their props are few, these vendors manage to create an individual feel with their own style and taste.

As I wander along the avenue with a keen eye for my own search, I pause to admire many varied items of interest. I can feel the devotion and commitment among the different sellers – imagine focusing your working life on a single type of object in the hope that someone shares your like-minded fascination.

The stamp collector offers baskets of soft-hued postage stamps in mint condition. Lengths of lace and ribbon are wound around torn bits of cardboard and arranged by colour and width. Madame Bronchart, with the linen nightdresses, has spent hours washing, bleaching and starching her inventory. The retired postman has sorted his postcards by date and scene. I fall prey to my regular *Paris Match* fix and am tempted by bunches of Louis XVI keys, not to mention the well-worn oak and iron combs used by an older generation of Provençals to collect blueberries.

The arrangement of a collection is as fundamental as the establishment. Knowing where to place objects and how to show them to advantage is the fun part. I believe that similar objects sit best together, and I arrange my collections by theme, by height, by size and even by colour. To arrange a new

PREVIOUS PAGE – My 'inspiration' wall and desk.
LEFT – Blue and white books, boxes and porcelain.

37

TOP - Emily wearing one of my 'vintage' sunhats.
RIGHT – The private dining room at La Mirande, Avignon.

collection or change an existing one means starting with a blank canvas; sometimes the most obvious of groupings only becomes clear when the slate is wiped clean. I remove each object from its home, lay them all out in a clear space and start from the beginning. A collection needs a backbone, so I always choose one object that will be my focus and then work until, to my eye, I have achieved a successful balance and harmony. The grouping of paintings or the placement of furniture works in much the same way.

The breadth and width of my collections have grown considerably since I moved to Provence, partly because loving this life and living this life mean by definition my collections have grown, and partly because I am as passionate about my home now as I was as a little girl. The objects I am fondest of are not of monetary value, they are a reflection of my life and my friendships. My collections are about gifts from my parents, a life of travel and change, relationships, the joys of parenthood and an eye for beauty. Every addition of an embroidered linen sheet or bronze photo frame, each gilt mirror or illustrated book that I hunt down, every shell collected on holiday with my children or anniversary gift from my husband means the collections become more emotionally significant. Periodically I declare that I will become a minimalist and rid my life of clutter, though I fear it is too late and would not only make for too tough a mental challenge but also be physically impossible to disentangle such an all-encompassing past.

Collecting is like a jigsaw puzzle: small, scrambled parts that only become whole when understood, identified and pieced together in entirety. Collections tell the story of life, provide the substance to ambience and are the very soul of the home.

—

RIGHT – A corner of the guest bedroom.
FOLLOWING PAGE – Emily's bedroom.

A SHOPPING LIST IS NOT FOR THE COLLECTOR – A COLLECTION OF OBJECTS SHOULD NOT BE A SET PIECE. COLLECTING IS ABOUT TAKING TIME AND KNOWING THAT THE REWARD IS NOT ALWAYS ABOUT THE ACQUISITION BUT WHAT IS DISCOVERED ON THE JOURNEY.

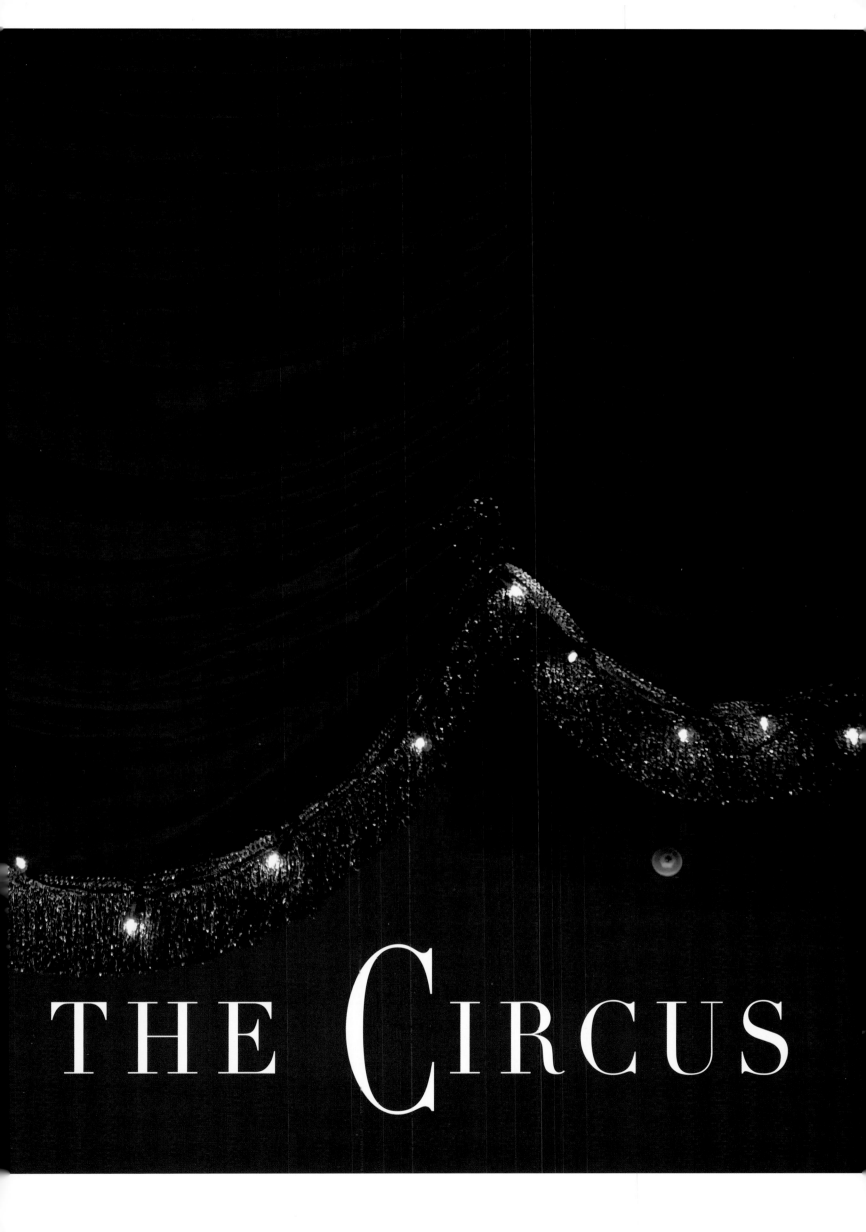

THE CIRCUS

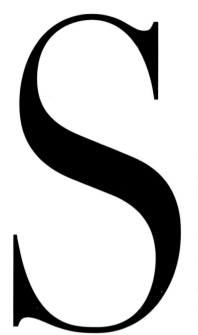

SUSPENDED HIGH ABOVE ME is a daring young woman on her flying trapeze. Dressed as a swashbuckling pirate, she swings with complete abandon, slicing through the air with only her physical strength to propel her. Her auburn hair is semi-hidden beneath a red bandana and her ruffled white shirt is nipped at the waist with a wide-buckled belt. Tucked into her waistband are a silver pistol and menacing sword. She wears mid-calf black leggings and soft leather pumps that give her feet the steel grip she needs. Overhead she fights her imaginary battles with flair and confidence. She is not attached to a harness or secondary rope and she does not swing over a safety net – Lady Pirate is gutsy, bold and fearless.

As she swings on her velvet-covered trapeze at high speed, turning inside out and upside down like a contortionist, the crowd holds its breath. We watch as she executes her complex manoeuvres, gasping and applauding each move but tentatively nervous for her next. Her silhouette against the star-painted canvas of the big top amplifies her every intrepid move. She is a star among stars.

SINCE THE EIGHTEENTH CENTURY crowds around the world have been entertained, enthralled and inspired by a visit to the circus – and I am no different. I want to be transported to a world of make believe and forget my grown-up responsibilities. I want to revel in the magical ambience of the circus and be filled with childlike wonder as the performers dazzle me with their talents.

In France there are more than 200 travelling circus groups. Cirque Stéphane Zavatta is a family-run troupe that travels to more than 300 towns and villages throughout France each year. They are easily distinguished by their red Kenworth prime movers and caravans. To keep their show on the road – all 450 tonnes of material, plus performers and animals – means a convoy of twenty-five vehicles and much manpower. To erect *le chapiteau* (the big top) with a seating capacity for 2000 requires more than a dozen men working over a four-hour period.

Driving into Perpignan, at the base of the Pyrénées in the Languedoc region of southern France, I cannot help but notice the posters on every street corner advertising Cirque Stéphane Zavatta. Cartoon-style, the big-top illustrations create a sense of expectation in the streets. A song resembling the melody of 'La Cucaracha' echoes in the distance – as I approach the site I discover the sounds are emanating from a promotional van for the circus. A larger-than-life resin clown is bolted to the roof of the van, and the dates and times for *le spectacle* are broadcast by loudspeaker. It is easy to follow the topsy-turvy red hat, big round nose and smiling wide mouth of the clown to *le chapiteau*.

A red trailer standing a good distance in front of the tent is painted with all the old circus favourites. Children line up with their parents at *la caisse* (the ticket box) to buy seats for the three o'clock matinee of 'Bel Canto'. I take three steps up to the glass window, buy a ticket and enter another world.

PREVIOUS PAGE – The Circus Bar, Montpelier.
LEFT – The clown on top of Cirque Stéphane Zavatta's van.

Le chapiteau is erected in the middle of the circus world. Around the perimeter the personal caravans, vehicles, trailers, four-by-fours and animal cages encircle and face the big top. Cirque Stéphane Zavatta is visually striking; every piece of equipment is designed to coordinate with the red-and-white stripes of the tent's exterior. For this circus family, their appearance on tour is as important as the show they perform, and the uniform design is a point of difference to distinguish them from other troupes.

As I enter *le chapiteau* my eyes must adjust to the soft lighting. The canvas above represents a night sky awash with stars, and the ring – the pulse of the circus – is surrounded by two rows of red velvet chairs. So close are these chairs to the action, like a box at the opera, it is as if I am sitting within the circle. Tiers of wooden benches rise up behind. A five-metre high metal cage encircles the ring in readiness for the renowned Stéphane Zavatta white tigers. Jewel-like laser patterns flash on the ceiling and Glen Miller swing plays in the background. The attendants ushering us to our seats are dressed in red military-style jackets with gold braiding, brass buttons and fringed epaulettes. The young girls selling popcorn and glow-in-the-dark wands for the children wear similar uniforms. Every partition of this 360-degree expanse is swathed in red velvet that is heavily trimmed with gold fringing. The curtains that conceal the backstage area are the same rich colour. It is a sumptuous and vibrant space.

As the lights dim a dry-ice machine fills the base of the ring with smoke and Monsieur Loyale, the French equivalent of a ringmaster, makes his first appearance. Wearing a red tailcoat, white shirt and black trousers, he welcomes the audience by way of a song he has composed especially for 'Bel Canto'. He is our master of ceremonies: he will introduce each act and provide some history about the circus and the artists along the way. It is his job to direct our attention and involve us in every part of today's performance. Our Monsieur Loyale is really Monsieur Hubert Bonnet, newly retired and a recent addition to the circus. As a child he adored everything about the circus and promised himself that when he took his retirement (in France this is normally at age sixty or sometimes younger) he would follow his heart. Monsieur Bonnet is an enthusiastic musician and singer, and as Monsieur Loyale he lives his childhood dream each day.

'*Bonjour tout le monde*,' (Hello everybody) he calls out with an infectious manner. '*Bonjour tout le monde*,' he repeats, this time louder, encouraging us to clap in time to the music. The spotlight roves around the tent, zapping the bright faces; the more we clap and laugh, the more excited and spontaneous Monsieur Loyale becomes. The circus atmosphere depends on the readiness of the audience to participate – the happier and more enlivened the crowd, the better the show.

To great applause Jimmy Klissing, *le patron* of the Stéphane Zavatta circus, makes his entrance alongside his renowned white Bengal tigers, Jerry and Heidi. Like his father and grandfather before him, Jimmy is an animal trainer. His tigers were born in captivity and have been hand-fed and raised by Jimmy. The affection between Jimmy and his tigers is obvious – a true love story.

Jerry and Heidi are faultless in their performance. Magnificent, beautiful creatures, they are regal in their posture and fluid in their movements. It was overwhelming to see these tigers close up and it is unimaginable to think they could be ferocious. Nevertheless, I am grateful for the cage.

The animals are an integral part of the live show, although in modern times attitudes toward animal performance have changed, and we may soon see this tradition phased out. While the animals add drama and tension to the performance, it is the clowns that really make or break the show. Circus clowns are multi-talented performers: they entertain and divert attention from the housekeeping side of things, but most importantly a good clown lightens the mood, refocuses lost attention and makes us laugh. At Cirque Stéphane Zavatta the Portuguese Herminio family do all of the above.

The Herminio family have been clowns for four generations. Monsieur Herminio was taught the secrets of Portuguese clowning by his father, and he is teaching his son and daughter the same traditions. It is not only the repertoires that are taught and passed on through the generations: some of the immaculate costumes in the Herminios' wardrobe are thirty years old.

André Herminio is seventeen and has been working with his parents since the age of five. André, a shy and timid teenager outside *le chapiteau*, turns into a crowd-pleaser the minute he runs

PREVIOUS PAGES – The exterior and the interior of 'Le Chapiteau'.
RIGHT – The children's soft toys, 'circus style'.

56

on stage. His face is made up clown-style and he wears red military garb with a matching beret tucked jauntily on one side of his dark hair. Oversized black boots make his feet appear two feet long. He amuses us with nothing more than a cute expression, a whistle and the tune made famous by comedian Benny Hill. His gestures and mannerisms are so exacting that he has a 'whistle language' we can easily understand and respond to. André manages to synchronise our clapping and make us comply with his every direction. He whistles up a pretty girl from the audience to participate in his mime show and extracts a kiss, much to the audience's delight. Grinning from ear to ear, he delivers her back to her boyfriend, winks and races off stage, only to return in seconds with a life-sized Raggedy Anne doll.

André's performance is about energy and momentum. After much slapping and clapping, the Raggedy Anne doll miraculously transforms to reveal a small girl, his sister, Raquel. At sixteen, she is still learning the ropes as an assistant. When her time comes for a starring role she will have no stage fright – it is as natural for Raquel to perform in front of an audience as it is to live with her family in a caravan and be forever on the move.

As a very cheeky André diverts our attention, the tigers' protective cage is removed and the ring prepared for the less dangerous acts – less dangerous for the audience, that is. Monsieur Loyale introduces Miss Cathy, and I watch mesmerised as she slithers serpent-like up a thick twisted rope, with what looks like the minimum of effort. She hangs suspended and somersaults from the rope in every direction, using the deftness of her limbs and her crampon-like grip to hold her weight. Her finale is stomach-turning: spinning madly, she secures the rope around her ankles and suddenly lets go with both hands to free fall, bungee-like, in front of us – stopping inches from the ground.

I feel giddy as I watch Miss Cathy spin, in awe of her flexibility and unflinching bravery. I am amazed by the lack of safety harness and protective netting in the ring. A trapeze or rope artist believes that if there is no risk there is no gain; these artists are like athletes, and to be put to the test is the difference between an amateur and a professional. Intuitively the artists are alive to the audience and appreciate complete concentration from them in order to perform to their highest standard. They depend on the audience for courage, and praise fuels their adrenalin.

Sitting so close to the inner circle means getting up close and personal with the animals. I make eye contact with the gorgeous elephant Indre, the mascot of Cirque Stéphane Zavatta, as she graciously sashays around the ring. She looks deeply into my eyes, bats to-die-for eyelashes and unfurls her mighty trunk to dust my jacket. She is in her element – an awesome girl who loves attention.

The camels, Eliott, Melino, Oudi and Tina, are even friendlier. Racing around and around the ring to the beat of an Indie pop song, they swing their long necks back and forth into the audience. Full, pouting lips and overactive jaws come towards those of us in the first few rows at great speed and regular intervals – it is hard not to flinch and strain back against the chairs.

The rest of the menagerie is very well behaved – even Otis the lama, who has been known to escape and enjoy an intimate mingle with the audience. Doctor Dolittle would be proud.

Following impressive showmanship, unbelievable feats of daring and inhuman shows of strength, it is for the Herminio clowns to close today's performance. Monsieur Herminio is the master of this act, with André and his mother the secondary players and Raquel in the wings as assistant. They are a multi-talented family with the responsibility of closing a great show, and they never falter. Radiant faces gaze back at this lovely family of clowns as we all enjoy the exuberant atmosphere in *le chapiteau*.

Monsieur Loyale thanks us for coming, in true French fashion with his hand held over his heart, and we clap all the artists for the final time as they parade around the ring.

This French circus is about family. They live together, work together and travel together – they are a 'firm' in themselves. The majority of the people working in Cirque Stéphane Zavatta are family members. They are born into the circus world and stay there. They are proud people and passionate ambassadors for their circus culture and artistic profession. Their spiritual home or heart is wherever *le chapiteau* is erected.

—

PREVIOUS PAGE – A daring and fearless performer swinging overhead.
LEFT AND RIGHT – André delighting the crowd with his antics.

65

I WANT TO BE TRANSPORTED TO A WORLD OF MAKE BELIEVE AND SPEND HOURS FORGETTING MY GROWN-UP RESPONSIBILITIES. I WANT TO REVEL IN THE MAGICAL AMBIENCE OF THE CIRCUS AND BE FILLED WITH CHILD LIKE WONDER AS THE PERFORMERS DAZZLE ME WITH THEIR TALENTS.

THE GARDEN

I AM NEVER SURE WHERE my garden begins and ends at Mas de Bérard. In my mind it is one and the same with the farm. All I know is that I have come to love both the garden around the *mas* and the groves of fruit trees with equal intensity.

During my adolescence and early twenties I thought very little about gardens – my interests were fashion and travel. I took the gardens of my homeland and the gardens of the countries I visited for granted and had little understanding of the knowledge, creativity and tireless effort that can be missed in a glance. But time changes all, and the exposures of childhood seep into our unconsciousness and creep up when we least expect it. For the last ten years in Provence I have thought of little else.

I have learnt much from the Provençal gardens around me. A Mediterranean influence makes them more colourful and wilder than the formal gardens of Paris. Varieties of plants in differing shades of green are planted side-by-side in beds and borders and clipped in a way that tells a story and forges a connection between them. When I look at the lavender beds, the olive trees and the vines I see layout and structure. Rows of cypress trees, avenues of plane trees and lines of espaliered apple trees are stalwart examples of balance and harmony.

Mas de Bérard had all the right ingredients to create my longed-for garden: 50 acres of reasonably flat land with enough established trees to give the garden the bones it needed. A canal running through the centre of the property and fed from the Alpilles mountains meant there would be no shortage of irrigation in the summer months.

The land was of differing make-up. One-third of the acreage was dry and rocky in true Provençal style, one-third was a rich and fertile oasis with an abundance of water, and the other third fell somewhere in between.

Where to start landscaping 50 acres? In the early days I confided in David a fear that we would never make the progress I so desperately wanted. I worried that the more I tried to go forward the more I went backward. He offered wise council, as is his nature: begin by working with small circles and expand outwards little by little; view the project in parts and tackle one area at a time. In his opinion, when I least expected, the parts would unite. He was right.

If I drew a map today of Mas de Bérard I would outline a square and divide it in three horizontal parts. The top portion of the map, nearest the mountains, would be devoted to olive trees growing in the arid limestone rocks. In the middle section, where the soil is rich and fertile, sits the house, garden and canal. The last part of my diagram would show lines of apple and pear trees. At the bottom of the square, in the centre, I would tack on a long rectangle to represent the plane-tree driveway.

The olive trees were the first stage in an ambitious scheme. Twenty acres had to be cleared, levelled and prepared for 3000 fledgling trees. We hoped the olive groves would be a beautiful addition and also one day make the farm self-supporting. Much care was taken to choose the varieties,

LEFT – The 'chicken shed'.
TOP – Iceberg roses and topiary bay trees leading to the swimming pool.

75

the distance they should be planted apart and the style of irrigation. The conditions were excellent for olives – the limestone rock, the dry scorching summer heat and often sub-zero winter temperatures. The trees, planted in lines and by varieties, stood no more than knee-high in April 2000; their stakes were the most robust and visible feature on the horizon. Nine birthdays later they pass over me and fill the once-untended land.

With our olive future prospering under the Provençal sun and the house restoration well underway, we started to plan for the garden around the *mas*. Our architect, Hugues Bosc, introduced us to landscape designer Michel Semini – as friends and colleagues for many years, they were in the habit of working together.

Michel spent many hours exploring the farm, studying the terrain and mulling over his ideas. Before we could even begin to discuss planting we had other more pressing structural issues to resolve – firstly, the positioning of a new driveway. We needed a road to connect the plane-tree driveway on one side of the property to the olive groves on the other. As with many details of the property, emotion, not practicality, ruled.

Hugues, Michel and I walked among the fields, taking in the view from all sides and gauging the most picturesque route. The land had been divided by rows of tall cypress trees, planted as a protective barrier against the forceful mistral wind. We needed to decide which of these trees could remain and which must be felled to make room for the driveway. Michel and Hugues had the imagination and experience to charter this road. They found it all so easy – a spray of orange paint marked the best and most cylindrical of the trees to be saved; a blast of green would determine those to be removed. Their assessment proved correct: the old plane-tree driveway that leads to and crosses a bridge over the canal was successfully extended to continue past the *mas*, traverse the property through the olive groves and exit on to Ancienne Voie Aurelia, the road that borders our property on the other side.

When the path was cleared for the driveway we set about selecting the perfect location for the swimming pool. We chose a site away from the house with a striking view of the mountains – the idea that the pool would be a separate destination from the other living areas.

With these practicalities underway, our thoughts could run to the non-existent garden in front of the house. Michel wanted to create equilibrium between what was established – the existing fruit trees and the infant olive grove – and the new garden, while also framing the backdrop for our view of the Alpilles mountains.

I am an inexperienced gardener with impractical dreams, whereas Michel is original and clever and combines these qualities with first-hand knowledge and real solutions. I was deaf to the problems of drainage and soil quality, completely lost amid talk of electrical circuits and lighting; levels and surveyors' studies were another language altogether. Michel managed these essential works with quiet confidence and efficiency.

When he presented his hand-coloured drawings of our soon-to-be garden my reaction was one of disbelief. Standing in a wasteland of builders' debris and equipment, I could scarcely picture this rich oasis of his imagination: schiaparelli-pink roses tumbling from walls and a trellis of 'Pierre de Ronsard'; wisteria and grapevines curling up and over an iron awning to provide shade on the terrace. He saw plane trees as parasols and gnarly olive trees as sculptures. Pomegranates would be the fruit trees to break the expanse of lawn and connect the new garden with the existing apple orchard. At the farthest point and on a higher level, Michel envisaged rows of lavender in the style of an amphitheatre, to lead the eye up over the distant olive groves and onwards to the mountains. We had earthmovers and tractors parked where he visualised stone ponds and running water. A derelict trough that once provided drinking water for the house was, in Michel's eye, a secret garden and gateway to the swimming pool. Michel's ideas flowed freely and he gave of himself generously and completely to our project.

Fast-forward seven years. Michel Semini's creation has taken hold and become one with the landscape. I see his footprint and his touch in every square inch, and I work hard to maintain his vision while injecting my own personality and touch. For a passionate landscaper such as Michel,

handing over his garden must have been like letting go of an adolescent child – a little sadness and fear mixed with much pride and happiness.

The garden has become my new best friend and I am impatient to expand and develop Michel's beginnings. As with my quest for aesthetic contentment inside the *mas*, I am forever looking for planting perfection on the outside. The more I plant, the more gaps I see; the more loveliness I see, the lovelier I want to make it.

My current obsessions are many. Roses, for their delicate but wise little faces – budding, blooming or blown, I am enamoured with them. Three beds of white iceberg roses are the focal point of the garden on the western side. I crave the seasonality of them – waiting for the first buds of spring and the feeling that summer is on the way, topping their heads regularly to have cut flowers for the *mas* from May to October and then pruning them back and settling them in for their winter slumber.

The climbing variety of iceberg throws a halo of blooms around the front door as they clamber up the stone walls; those that tumble from the cypress trees splash a shock of white among the leafy apple orchards. These climbers are prolific growers in the Provençal climate, and their lack of uniformity sits well in a farm garden. Our hot-pink rose – affectionately renamed the 'Shocking Semini' because neither Michel nor I can remember her correct title – is thick and dense and blooms less frequently than the iceberg. Like a contemporary painting this rose makes a simple statement in a complex landscape. The wooden pergola of 'Pierre de Ronsard' is the charmer of this garden; the sensual appearance and heady scent is an open invitation to stroke the velvety petals.

The iris is very Provence; the clumps of orchid-like bulbs typify the countryside so loved by Van Gogh and Cézanne. These grow in the wild but not in abundance at Mas de Bérard; to introduce them and watch them multiply is my mission. I have planted hundreds of white irises in scattered drifts around the farm to safeguard the true feel of Provence. I am grateful for the life I have found and am conscious of the generosity of a country that has welcomed me – it is only right that I watch over the land around me.

Almond trees occupy my thoughts for the same reason. Once upon a time there were extensive almond orchards throughout Provence, but now there are very few. I have begun a program to plant almond trees across the width of our property. With scrappy foliage and weak-looking limbs, an almond tree is easy to miss, but when it blossoms and heralds the arrival of spring, it is a prince in Provence.

The French addiction to structure and form is alive and well at Mas de Bérard. I am hooked on this habit of shearing and shaping a myriad evergreen shrubs to configure living sculptures. Spirals, triangles, spheres and pyramids are contrasts in form and volume. The resuscitation of a dishevelled bay tree into a clean and upstanding member of the garden is a joy to behold. Ahmed, our part-time gardener and shaper of all shapes, has a deadeye and deft hand with the clippers. He trims every hedge and topiary by hand with immaculate precision. I watch his technique and have learnt his secret – he takes time, he stands back to check his progress, he works in sections and follows his line.

I VIEW THE GARDEN AS A SERIES OF EXTERIOR ROOMS. Moving between areas provides an element of surprise and a changing palette for outdoor living. I like to have specific destinations in the garden for eating, reading, sleeping and swimming. The garden surrounding the house is lush and verdant, whereas the swimming pool is some distance away from the *mas* and is sparse and rugged in atmosphere. The pool is accessed via a secret garden; a small path leads from the lawn into this intimate courtyard that is paved with fine powder-like gravel and interspersed with slabs of stone. In the French way, the planting is simple but structured; contrasts are achieved with leaf texture and shades of green. A solid limestone wall forms the backdrop to this hidden garden, hiding the pool from the house and providing privacy and remoteness.

RIGHT – Pierre de Ronsard roses blooming over a wooden trellis.
FOLLOWING PAGES – The Persimmon tree brushed with snow.
The hidden courtyard that marks the entrance to the swimming pool.

When I swim I feel as if I am skimming through the lines of olive trees, with only the Alpilles mountains and the endless sky for company. Within this enclosure the summer temperatures are more intense, the cicada buzz is louder and the outlying fields shimmer in the heat.

In Provence, where to eat, where to lounge and where to nap depends on the month and the position of the sun. I arrange the furniture to capture the sun or the shade and to encourage laziness. In July and August life convenes under the wisteria-clad awning of the terrace because it is simply too hot to be anywhere else – except in the swimming pool. From September to October the heat is less sapping and activity moves to the lawn. I set up tables and chairs for lunch beside the lavender amphitheatre or underneath the umbrella-like plane trees; the sofas, I group around the garden. Curling up with a good read or having a quiet snooze seems the perfect pastime in the garden. In November, December and January the furniture is stored and the idle hot days of summer are relegated to memory, but come late March and April, the garden opens her doors and the furniture parade starts over.

A GARDEN IS AN OPEN BOOK and can be read by anyone who chooses to turn the pages. It is also a reflection of the temperament and personality of its owner and can pronounce much about character. Committed gardeners give of their heart and soul to create their personal paradise. They understand that the establishment, growth and maturity of a garden are akin to friendship – the more we give the more we gain. Gardens require nurturing to establish a solid foundation, and both time and attention to blossom – not unlike the friends we hold dear.

David was right: the circumference of my circle has widened and the separate parts are gradually meshing. The plane-tree driveway and the apple and pear orchards that I fell in love with in 1999 are waiting for attention. They are very much a part of the whole picture and, somewhat dishevelled, in many ways they are the most endearing parts of the property – the reminder of how things began.

Which part of the garden is my favourite? If asked in November I would answer without hesitation: the olive groves. If I thought about this in April I would have to say the apple orchard. In May I would opt for the iris garden. But now I have neglected to mention the climbing roses, the beds of icebergs and the amphitheatre of lavender. In truth I am devoted to every part of this evolving canvas. A garden lives and breathes when there is a true appreciation and deep understanding between nature and individuals.

COMMITTED GARDENERS GIVE
OF THEIR HEART AND SOUL
TO CREATE THEIR PERSONAL
PARADISE. THEY UNDERSTAND
THAT THE ESTABLISHMENT,
GROWTH AND MATURITY OF A
GARDEN ARE AKIN TO FRIENDSHIP
– THE MORE WE GIVE THE MORE
WE GAIN.

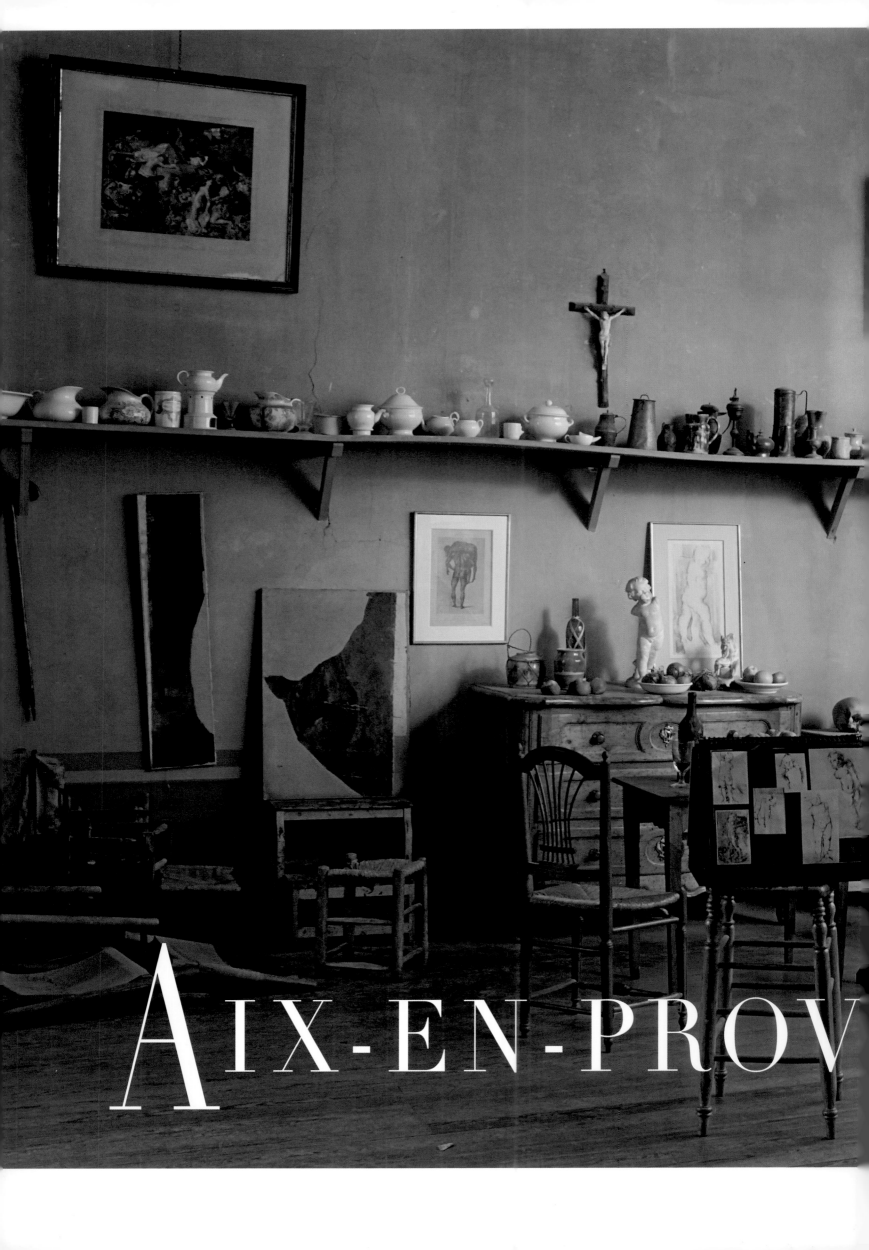

AIX-EN-PROV

ENCE

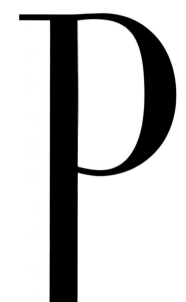

POST-IMPRESSIONIST PAINTER PAUL CÉZANNE felt deeply the connection between his local geography and his garden. During his career he made spasmodic trips to study in Paris, but he always returned home to Aix-en-Provence. The vitality of the countryside, the brilliance of the Provençal light and the dominating Mont Sainte Victoire captured his imagination and were never far from his thoughts.

I often make the forty-minute trip from Saint-Rémy-de-Provence to Aix-en-Provence, and each time I drive along the A7 *autoroute* I too am fascinated by this compelling mountain. With an altitude of 1011 metres, this symbol of Provence lies like a sleeping giant, dominating the town and the surrounding landscape. The countryside is a kaleidoscope of colour: silvery olive trees, chartreuse vineyards, blue-black pine trees and 'velvet' green grasses. When the soaring sky is empty of clouds, the occasional ploughed field seems unnaturally rich in colour. This is Cézanne's palette – blues, greens, yellows and oranges. For me, to discover Cézanne is to discover Aix-en-Provence, and vice versa.

Known as the city of a thousand fountains, Aix-en-Provence was founded over thermal springs by the Romans in 123 BC and is now a thriving university town and learning centre. The main boulevard, the Cours Mirabeau, is easily distinguishable by the fountain La Rotonde, and is my preferred gateway to the town. La Rotonde has a distinctly Parisian feel: a deciding presence and a sense of celebration. This circular pond is decorated with swans, lions, angels and dolphins. A central pedestal holds three sculptures that represent agriculture, the arts and the justice system. Water, the heart of this town's history, sprouts, gurgles and cascades from all sides.

An avenue of plane trees separates the old district of Aix from the new. One side of this wide street is lined with cafes and the other with offices and banks. Many fine old stone houses, yellow-gold in colour and pretty in their architectural detail, blend into this commercial mix, giving Aix a sophisticated, urban feel.

Each time I approach the town centre by way of the Cours Mirabeau and drive around La Rotonde I am filled with excitement – the feeling at the beginning of a well-planned and anticipated day out. I have a pattern to my days in Aix, habit I suppose. Unintentionally I follow the same routine: I have a coffee (or lunch) at Les Deux Garçons, poke my head into Musée Granet (or any other exhibition of interest), I browse the market, I buy flowers and spend the afternoon with a shopping list for the *mas* or gift-buying for birthdays and holidays, with perhaps a visit to the famed Le Chocolaterie de Puyricard.

LES DEUX GARÇONS was one of Cézanne's favoured eateries. Dining here is not so much about the food but about soaking up the local history and enjoying the atmosphere. When I approach Les Deux Garçons I cannot help but imagine artists such as Cézanne and Picasso at *apéritif*

LEFT AND RIGHT – Les Deux Garçons, Aix-en-Provence.

hour drinking, debating and gazing out on the Cours Mirabeau from their sidewalk table. I wonder whether Emile Zola, Cézanne's childhood friend, wrote here or whether Ernest Hemingway penned a word on a break from Paris. The guest list is a veritable who's who of literary history.

Les Deux Garçons follows the same routine as the Parisian cafe: waiters race back and forth taking orders and presenting food to diners jammed together at tiny tables, sharing intimate space with their neighbors. The linen-covered outdoor tables face the street and provide an uninterrupted view of the passing parade – university students, glamorous girls out and about, buskers and businessmen. What indoor dining lacks in atmosphere it makes up for with decor. Red damask curtains over the doorway invite the diner into a world of early-nineteenth-century *époque consulaire*: painted wooden panelling, gilt mirrors and ornate ceilings. The bottle-green leather banquette offers the perfect place to sip away and people-watch in the reflections around the room.

Musée Granet on the Place Saint-Jean-de-Malte was established in 1838 and named in honour of painter François Marius Granet, who was born in Aix-en-Provence and upon his death bequeathed the majority of his collection to the town. Since 1984 Musée Granet has acquired eight paintings by Cézanne, not only to showcase Aix-en-Provence as Cézanne's birthplace and home but also to promote international recognition for the museum and its benefactor. The permanent exhibition comprises works from sixteenth- and seventeenth-century French, Dutch, Flemish and Italian artists. Not-to-be-missed works are the 1807 portrait of François Granet by Ingres, a French neoclassical portrait painter, and the beautifully lit sculpture gallery.

AIX-EN-PROVENCE is not only a town of history, art and culture. Small boutiques cater for every taste, and the market is well underway by nine o'clock three mornings a week. The market stretches throughout the town and occupies many of the public squares. There is Place des Prêcheurs devoted to fruit and vegetables, and Place Richelme for meat and fish. In front of the town hall in Place de Verdun are the second-hand dealers (including my preferred bookseller, Monsieur Culat) who offer books, magazines, vinyl records, antique jewellery, china and cutlery. Close by is the Rue Monclar, where fashion, furs or bikinis can be found depending on the time of year, and the itinerant travellers sell cashmere scarves and silk sarongs from India and Pakistan. Further along are the household appliances and fabrics. My usual route takes me past the vendors offering fish, ducks, rabbits, chickens, fruit, jams and scented honey until I reach my destination: the flower market at Place de l'Hotel de Ville.

I make the trek from Saint-Rémy-de-Provence fortnightly to feast my eyes on the selection and buy for the *mas*. The choice is vast, and because the market runs three days a week the flowers are always fresh and seasonal. Buying flowers at the market is refreshing after the florists or supermarkets in urban centres, where most of the flowers are imported and kept alive in a cool room. I look forward to what the growers have to offer each month, and no two visits are the same. Unlike clothes shopping, flower buying puts me in the best mood: I always find something I like, I never have to try them on, they look beautiful and the price tag won't burn the bank. It is a win–win experience.

I never approach the market with a plan; I like to decide on the spot which flowers I will take home. This involves a long conversation, because in France there is always time for talk of ideas and helpful hints. It goes something like this . . . The initial good morning, exchange of pleasantries and mention of the weather (always yesterday's, today's and tomorrow's forecast). Then I ask my first question: Where were the flowers grown, and how long will they last? Now my accent will be detected and it will be the vendor's turn for a question: Where am I from and why am I in France? I try to explain my complicated living arrangements, which sparks interest; the French love Australians and especially ones who love France. After I mention I live in Saint-Rémy-de-Provence there are many more questions, to which I am happy to respond: How many children? What about my family? Why France? It is only

after this exchange that we get down to the business of flowers. These gentle conversations about not much at all are like therapy in our hurried world.

In France flowers are sold by colour. The green-white anemones sitting in buckets alongside the red and blue bunches look patriotic – a coincidental play on the blue, white and red. The tulips are arranged in a colour wave of pink, peach, rose, mauve and lilac. The lilies are in every shade from salmon-pink to magenta-red. There are trestle tables of bulbs, tables of orchids, pots of geraniums and buxus topiaries for the gardeners. The only limitation to my shopping is the problem of carrying my purchases, keeping them alive, and the distance between the markets and my car. It pays to arrive early and park undercover not far from this side of town. I bring bottles of water and plastic buckets to hold the flowers in the car boot until I get home.

By one o'clock it is over. All that remains of the morning's commerce are the washed-down stone squares and cobbled streets. Ten minutes of sunshine later, it is as if the market never existed.

MY AIX-EN-PROVENCE is all about the sensory delights. Le Chocolaterie de Puyricard on the Rue Rifle-Rafle is a family-owned business specialising in handmade chocolates and sweets. Master *chocolatiers* use the finest and freshest ingredients to create their chocolates in their factory several kilometres outside Aix-en-Provence. The chocolates are made on demand and, as luck would have it (for greedy girls like me), the chocolates must be eaten with no time to waste. Le Chocolaterie de Puyricard offers nearly a hundred hand-dipped, moulded chocolates, soft fruit pastilles, glacé chestnuts, almonds and caramels, plus Puyricard's own *calissons*.

Aix-en-Provence is the home of the *calisson*, the traditional French sweet made of ground almonds and a fruit paste of melon and orange, finished with a thin layer of white icing. Biting into a *calisson* is not unlike biting into marzipan, although the flavour is much sweeter because of the fruit. Almond-shaped and presented in gift boxes, they are bought and eaten by the French at holiday time, especially Christmas.

Inside the shop the chocolates – dark, bitter and milk selections with centers of mandarin, orange and raspberry, and names such as Agnes, Madeleine, Isabelle and Christelle – are presented in glass cases with caramel, coffee and praline truffles. There are violet crèmes, nougats and liqueur-filled bites but no white chocolates at Puyricard. (White chocolate is not 'true' chocolate because the cocoa, which adds flavour and colour, has been removed in the reduction process.) As I make my selection and watch the white-gloved hand of the assistant dart in and out of the cabinets, I enjoy a Willy Wonka moment for grown-ups.

ALONG WITH THE DELIGHTS of Le Chocolaterie de Puyricard, the Musée Granet, the many shops and galleries and the markets in the centre of town, Aix-en-Provence also offers visitors the unique experience of immersing themselves in the life and work of Paul Cézanne: his family home at Jas de Bouffan, his studio at Les Lauves and Mont Saint Victoire on the outskirts of the town.

Jas de Bouffan is approached via a plane-tree-lined driveway, under-planted with pale blue irises and rambling roses. Cézanne re-created much of the surrounds on canvas: the mature gardens, the ornate fountain and simple pond, the orangery and the six outbuildings are some of his best-known images. He lived at Jas de Bouffan until the death of his father and in 1899 he and his sisters sold the property. In 1994 the house passed to the city of Aix and will one day be opened as a museum. Cézanne's home is no longer the haven of peace and tranquillity it was when he was growing up, nor is it in the countryside – a hundred years of progress have brought the urban touch right outside Jas de Bouffan's iron gates.

LEFT – Chocolates from Le Chocolaterie de Puyricard, Aix-en-Provence.

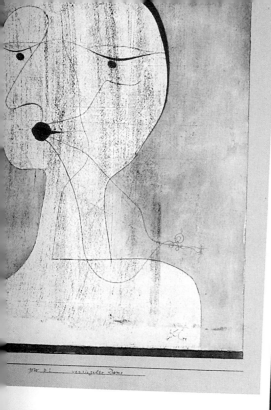

In 1901 Cézanne purchased half an acre at Les Lauves in the foothills of Mont Saint Victoire. Here he continued his love affair with the mountain and created his atelier and garden close by. The spacious atelier was furnished simply and drenched in morning sunlight. This generous space, away from his home in the centre of Aix-en-Provence, enabled him to paint large-scale works and arrange chosen objects for his still-life compositions. Cézanne would select apples, aged for some months in order to capture on canvas their changing state of decay, and place them alongside simple tableware and linens. His pottery bowls, pewter jugs and porcelain were artfully displayed on a long wooden shelf above a Provençal commode. Such simple objects were the impetus for his genius. Closing my eyes in Les Lauves, I can truly feel his presence and almost detect the heady scent of turpentine, oil paint and over-ripe apple.

Cézanne had many reasons to be passionate about Les Lauves, the main being that he was submerged in landscape, with no distinction between his garden and the nature outside: the olive groves, fruit orchards and the views of farmhouses, cliffs, trees and branches.

I believe that to stand in Cézanne's studio, among his easels, paintboxes and props, where he painted some of his finest works during the last years of his life, and to drive or hike around Mont Saint Victoire, perhaps even climb to the top, is to know and find the spirit of Paul Cézanne. To understand Cézanne is to understand the countryside of Provence.

RIGHT – Cézanne's paint boxes.
FOLLOWING PAGE – Cézanne's still life recreated in his studio.

BY ONE O'CLOCK IT IS OVER. ALL THAT REMAINS OF THE MORNING'S COMMERCE ARE THE WASHED-DOWN STONE SQUARES AND COBBLED STREETS. TEN MINUTES OF SUNSHINE LATER, IT IS AS IF THE MARKET NEVER EXISTED.

W HITE

T here is a secret side to Provence, a 'white' Provence that is sometimes forgotten in the rush to smell the lavender or admire the sunflowers. It is the Provence of white light, powder-puff clouds and silver lightning strikes. White is a symbol of peace and the sign to surrender – nothing more apt could apply to life in Provence, a peaceful existence and an easy surrender.

WHEN I THINK 'WHITE' I think of the magical light in Provence. It washes over the landscape with a clarity that makes everything crystal clear. Walking in the mountains behind Mas de Bérard, the light plays tricks with my eyes and my familiar subjects change under close scrutiny. The blue sky recedes into nothingness, pushed away by the sun's forceful rays, and the limestone paths grow luminescent in relief against the native foliage. The mountain paths are made up of broken gravel chips of all shapes and sizes. Close up these stones are a multitude of colours – every shade of beige and grey imaginable – yet when I look ahead I see only startling white.

On either side of the path wildflowers spill out from the *garrigue*, the rugged plant life of the mountains. Baby powder-white heads with button centres jostle for their place alongside the hardier rosemary, thyme and wild oak. Every now and then I see the occasional dandelion – their gossamer heads are so much larger than the ones I recall from childhood; I think it would be impossible to blow their fluffy tops clean away with a single breath. On my right, the rows of vines planted in this uneven terrain pale into insignificance as the light bleaches their vivid leaves and highlights the rocky beds.

Winding my way home, I cross the Ancienne Voie Aurelia, enter our property and walk down the driveway through the olive groves. The trees are in bud and I cross my fingers that in the coming weeks the trees will blossom and pollinate without any hindrance from the elements. As I cut through the fruit trees towards the house I see only a mass of white: the iceberg roses, in full bloom.

WHEN I THINK 'WHITE' I think of the one day of the year in Provence on which the colours of the landscape – the earthy oranges, the ochre yellows, the brilliant blues and the luscious greens – are forgotten and white takes centre stage: the 1st of May.

La Fête du Muguet is celebrated on France's Labour Day holiday. The French celebrate the arrival of spring by presenting family and friends with a sprig of lily-of-the-valley, to wish them happiness. This year the season feels as if it has truly arrived in Saint-Rémy-de-Provence and I have that

definite spring-in-the-step feeling that comes after a lengthy winter and months of semi-hibernation at home.

Lulu, whose invaluable help keeps all things running smoothly at the *mas*, bounces through the door with her indefatigable energy and announces she has come to deliver happiness and good luck. She has in her hands a bouquet of lily-of-the-valley that trails a scent so heavenly I cannot stop inhaling the sweet perfume. Lulu is making the rounds with her delicate bunches and spreading good wishes to her parents, sister and friends – she is a kind of May Day Santa.

In all my French years I have never before been in Saint-Rémy-de-Provence for La Fête du Muguet. The village is crowded with tourists taking advantage of a long weekend and locals surfacing from their winter retreat to enjoy the sunshine. This is the one day of the year in France that anyone can sell flowers without a licence, so in true French fashion many locals have come to sell not only lily-of-the-valley but other flowers and plants in the town square – in France any excuse calls for a market. Springtime is infectious and is evident in the body language of the people strolling around the village. Girls of all ages clutch a stem or two of this white good-luck charm and tilt their heads to breathe in the fragrance deeply; it is hard to believe that such a petite flower could be so potent. Although the irony of this public holiday – a day to celebrate work while not working – has not escaped me, I find this flower-giving as a way to wish the world well an adorable custom.

It is impossible to escape this white mood, so buying pots of lily-of-the-valley seems like the thing to do. I will find a shady place in the garden to plant these bulbs so I am well prepared for La Fête du Muguet next year. Walking among this exquisite scent in the spring sunshine, so welcome after the months of frosty mornings and chilly mistral winds, makes the seriousness of life evaporate. This May Day I can think of no place I would rather be.

WHEN I THINK 'WHITE' I think of the delicious tastes and textures of the food in Provence: coconut ice-cream and melt-in-the-mouth meringues from Bar Roma in the village . . . *calissons* from Aix-en-Provence and fat bars of nougat from Montpellier . . . *fleur de sel*, the crunchy white flakes so appropriately named 'flower of salt' and much softer to the palette than regular salt . . . mushrooms, all varieties scrutinised in the markets like precious jewels for imperfections, and fresh garlic, plaited like a hairpiece and hanging high from a portable clothing rail. There is nothing like a good drop of Vieux Télégraphe white wine from the vineyards of Châteauneuf-du-Pape and the tingle of bubbles from a sip of champagne. And bread: the I-shouldn't-eat-white-bread-every-day bread that is so light to the touch and taste that it almost doesn't count.

WHEN I THINK 'WHITE' I think of the old men driving past me on the Ancienne Voie Aurelia in their beat-up white Peugeot vans, their wayward mutts sitting beside them on the front seat, yapping madly and impatient for a run. These cute little vans have a protruding bonnet and small, round, wide-set headlights, which give them the appearance of a dog's snout – the van and the dog seemed to have morphed together.

WHEN I THINK 'WHITE' I think of serenity and the dearest little children dressed as angels dancing hand in hand in the village Christmas pageant. Thinking of them makes me wistful and I reminisce for a time not so long ago when Emily, Venetia and Paddy were young enough to perform in concerts and plays. As the holidays draw near, I immediately picture the garden and the

LEFT – The table set for breakfast in the apple orchard at Mas de Bérard.
TOP – Meringues from Bar Roma, Saint Rémy de Provence. My collection of linen nighties.

127

olive trees at Mas de Bérard blanketed in snow, and a white Christmas. With this image in mind I begin to imagine trimming the tree with my treasured decorations.

W HEN I THINK 'WHITE' I think of design. Andrée Putnam is a French icon of interior design – a living example that style knows no age or bounds. Often thought of as the Coco Chanel of interior designers, her work philosophy and infallible eye mean that her designs are in rhythm and harmony where function and comfort are of the utmost importance. I have found her simple interiors with neutral backgrounds and her arrangements of objects that are different in nature and varied in style a great reference point when it comes to arranging my own furniture and objects at Mas de Bérard. From Putnam I have learnt that the objects in a room must relate and work together to create a united impression, somewhat like fashion. For fashion to demonstrate style and individual flair, pieces must compliment each other but need not necessarily match perfectly or be the work of a single creator. Interior design follows the same formula, and an interior space, like a fashion wardrobe, must not only be visually pleasing and tailored to the individual but be practical as well.

The use of contrasting tones between the white palettes in some of our living spaces at the *mas* provides a calm haven and simple backdrop for the setting in which we live. The terrace, furnished simply with forged-iron sofas and oversized white cushions, makes the garden and the Alpilles mountains beyond our focal point.

Andrée Putnam's design philosophies are inherent. The rebel spirit of her childhood sparked her quest for original design, a need to empty rooms and forgo the heavier French antiques and wood panelling of her youth, to re-create spaces and make beautiful things. Putnam believes that anything can be luxurious as long as 'there is a style, a point of view'. I could not agree more.

W HEN I THINK 'WHITE' I think of comfort. My idea of comfort is a very long soak in an old-style enamel bathtub after a hard day's work, the water foaming with bubbles and the knowledge that the thick, fluffy white towel is warmed and ready nearby. It is my white embroidered linen nightdress at the end of the bed and the all-encompassing white bathrobe. Comfort is slipping between deliciously crisp white sheets on a freezing night, finding a hot water bottle at the foot of the bed and the feeling of abandonment as my head hits the light-as-a-feather pillow. Comfort must feel luxurious, pamper the body and ease the mind – a way of tuning out and turning off.

The simple pleasures are truly the most extravagant and the most luxurious. I find that at Mas de Bérard a mood can alter miraculously with flowers or a scented candle. A posy of iceberg roses hand-picked from the garden and placed by the bedside or on the dressing table is soothing for the spirit and a feast for the eyes. The 'Casablanca lily' scented candle that burns close by as I write throws an ambience that helps my productivity and concentration. Every day I arrange a bunch of flowers or a single bloom beside me as I work – today it is a long-stemmed white phalaenopsis orchid on my desk. When I struggle to find the right word or phrase to best express my sentiments I can focus on something of beauty and take my time.

I believe that these simple gestures and attention to detail are what make my home my castle. Home should be an oasis; the one true bolthole of security and the one place you always feel a slight misgiving to leave. Home is about that excited feeling deep inside when you unlock the door after an absence, fall over yourself to dump the bags, and race around breathing in the familiar. Home is the place to spend time and create ambience.

COMFORT IS SLIPPING BETWEEN DELICIOUSLY CRISP
WHITE SHEETS ON A FREEZING NIGHT, FINDING A HOT
WATER BOTTLE AT THE FOOT OF THE BED AND THE
FEELING OF ABANDONMENT AS MY HEAD HITS THE
LIGHT-AS-A-FEATHER PILLOW. COMFORT MUST FEEL
LUXURIOUS, PAMPER THE BODY AND EASE THE MIND –
A WAY OF TUNING OUT AND TURNING OFF.

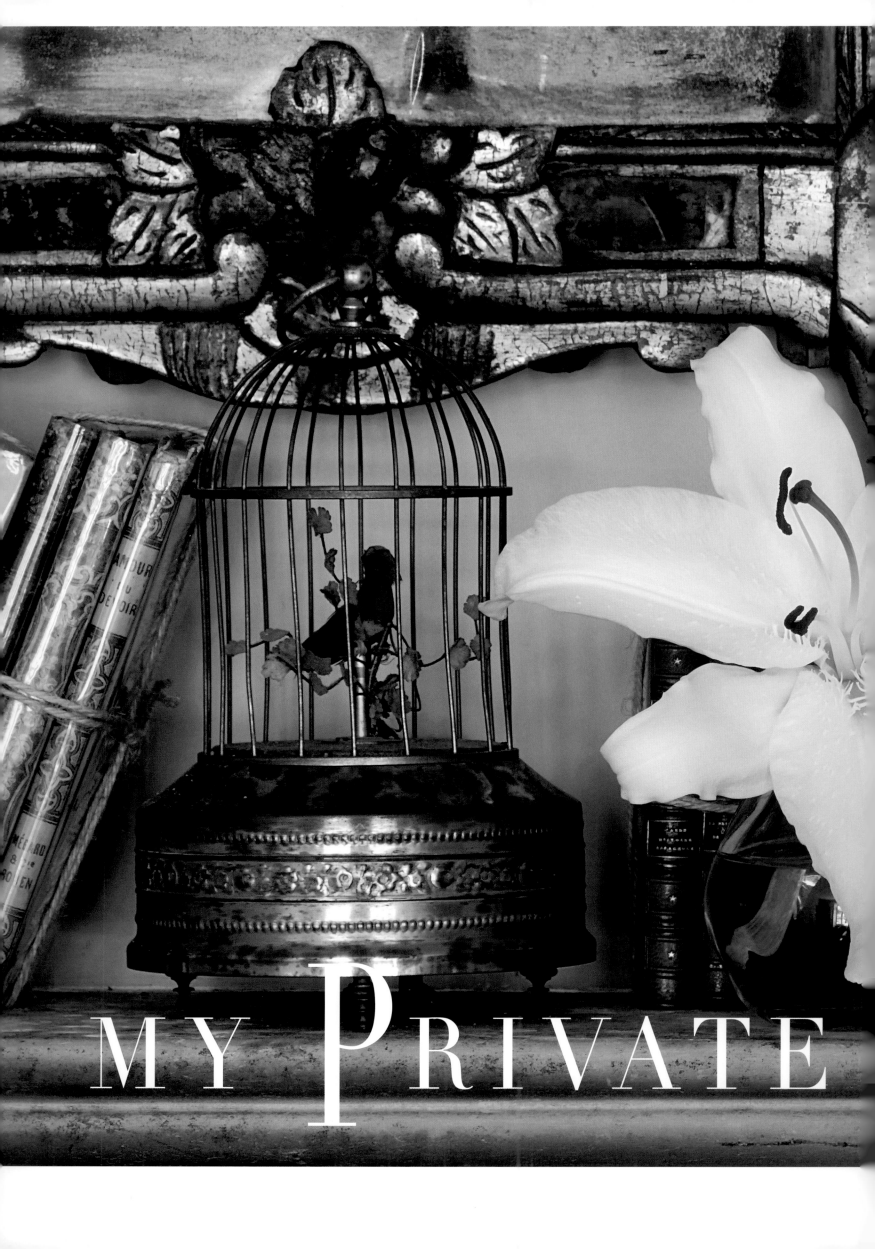

MY PRIVATE

PROVENCE

AT THE MENTION OF PROVENCE most people's eyes light up with thoughts of sunshine and lazy days by the Mediterranean or images of picturesque hilltop villages and Roman ruins. Made up of several *départements* in southern France – the Var, the Vaucluse, the Bouches-du-Rhône, some of the Alpes-de-Haute-Provence and the Alpes-Maritimes – Provence is all this and more.

When the proper noun 'Provence' turns into an adjective she becomes a type of cuisine and a form of interior decoration. Provençal cooking is all about seasonal availability and freshness with a strong emphasis on seafood due to coastal proximity. Garlic, parsley and a copious pouring of olive oil are obligatory in every recipe. Provençal interior decoration is immediately recognisable by its country flavour, a relaxed and slightly shabby-chic look. It is a diverse mix of furnishings, in which the rustic may well sit next to the contemporary, the painted or the fine. In the past bright and busy cottons were the face of Provence, but now neutral linens and pattern-free fabrics are increasingly popular. Multiple shades of taupe and the occasional stripe are the new alternative to prints of cicadas, olives and grapes. Provence is both a geographical definition and a way of life.

Provence is individual for everyone. A visit to the old town of Nice will leave an entirely different impression than a visit to the old port of Marseille, and a day in Aix-en-Provence is a world away from a day in St-Tropez. As you move through Provence you will notice perceptible changes in the landscape and the architecture – each village has its own unique flavour. I live in the Bouches-du-Rhône, could not imagine living anywhere else and am fiercely loyal to the Alpilles (the informal namesake of my piece of Provence). Those who live in the Luberon, in the heart of the Vaucluse, are equally unwavering and I am sure could not imagine life elsewhere. The truth is that to spend a day, a month or a lifetime in any region of Provence is, to my mind, good fortune.

As I jog alongside the canal, which meanders through our property towards the villages of Eygalières in one direction and Saint-Etienne-du-Grès in the other, I sometimes think about what Provence really means to me, about all the changes I have made in the last ten years – new countries, further travel and the many people I have encountered.

My private journey into Provence has been one of discovery. I have learnt that a new life in a foreign land is not only exciting, challenging and life-altering, but more importantly it is a fresh beginning. Embracing something unfamiliar means that the adventure never ends, and it is the discoveries I make on this adventure that keep me asking questions and searching for answers. Facing change keeps my mind flexible, and I believe that to be open to new ideas and experiences is one of the most important qualities to possess. It is my good fortune and advantage to be an observer of, and at the same time to be immersed in, Provence. This immersion has reinforced my personal philosophy that home and family are all-important, and at the same time fed my curiosity for interiors and enabled me to educate my tastes in the French way. As my exposure to French life grows, I learn more and more how to create this eclectic style of decorating and ambience in my own home.

PREVIOUS PAGE – The view through olive groves towards the ruins of Les Baux de Provence.
LEFT – Venetia in the garden at Mas de Bérard.

A discovery is often made because of a chance encounter. I am inquisitive by nature and am always intrigued by what I don't know or haven't seen. I think I am a cup-half-full kind of person, which is perhaps why I always believe I will stumble upon the fabulous find in the antique market, unearth the Roman coin somewhere in our fields or miss out on something extraordinary if I don't explore every possibility and chase every lead.

Such a chance encounter came about during one of my many visits to the olive mill CastelaS, where I take our olives to be pressed. Jean-Benoît Hugues, the proprietor, introduced me to another patron, and the three of us started chatting. We talked of olives of course, life in Provence and our individual histories. My fellow patron invited me to join him for tea and see, in his humble opinion, one of the 'most spectacular views' in Les Baux-de-Provence. Armed with a set of loose directions, I arranged to visit within the half-hour. It was a difficult property to find, but as I crawled up the winding dirt road, pulling over several times to enjoy the view, I had to agree that the aspect was as promised. Many wrong turns and some forty minutes later I was standing on a terrace with a breathtaking vista across olive groves and vineyards.

The stone house was hunkered into the hillside and as I climbed the steps to this hidden gem I thought how glad I was that I had followed my intuition and taken up this invitation. Living in Provence has made me less reserved and more amenable; I am not sure that in my past life I would have chased up hillsides for the promise of a view and a cup of tea with a stranger, but a shared love of Provence brings out a common bond.

We drank tea in a room whose interior was as enchanting as the view from the terrace. Smouldering embers from the night before lent a haziness to the atmosphere: paintings on the walls, sculptures on the bookcases, sunk-in sofas, wax-covered candlesticks, endless books and magazines . . . I wanted to curl up there and then. I could easily imagine the long lazy dinners and lively conversations that took place around the generous table. Well worn and well loved, this home was real, not decorated or styled.

I AM AN INTERIORS JUNKIE. I need no excuse to talk about style, decoration or furniture. I flick through as many shelter magazines as I can find and I am forever searching for the latest design books or reading my daily blogs. And this is how I can discover what is sometimes right under my nose.

La Maison du Village is in the centre of Saint-Rémy-de-Provence, halfway down a charming street with the unlikely name of Rue du 8 Mai 1945. (A historical tongue twister in any language, so fortunately the hotel is not difficult to find with a local map.) Guests enter from the street into a long rectangular salon. A stone chimneybreast at the end of this room leads the eye past a narrow curving staircase to the private domain upstairs. This converted eighteenth-century village house is a small boutique hotel that is about as non-hotel as I know. The mood is relaxed and informal – last-people-to-bed-please-lock-the-door-and-turn-off-the-lights kind of informality.

The sitting room and dining room are painted a beetle-nut red and both face a gravelled courtyard. Outside, small round tables and chairs with soft aubergine-coloured cushions are arranged around a stone fountain; the tinkling sound of water and a few soft chirps are the only sounds to interrupt the peace and quiet. Throughout the reception rooms is a mix of soft furnishings in various textures and shades of chocolate, burgundy and plum. The paintings, mirrors and lighting are all pleasing to the eye, but it is not one particular part of the styling that works for me, it is the strong use of colour and the overall impression that appeals to me. The decor at La Maison du Village is brave, and the small spaces make big statements.

The bedrooms are a blend of the old and the contemporary, with the same bold use of colour. Well-worn terracotta floors, shuttered windows, narrow corridors and curving stairs are pure

PREVIOUS PAGES – 'Private Provence' in the village of Fontvielle.
RIGHT – The kitchen at Mas de Bérard.

144

Provence. The upholstery and furniture are in marvellous contradiction – violet and pink velvet-covered Louis-style bedheads and armchairs. The names of the bedrooms are delicious: La Suite Violette, La Chambre Rose, La Suite Framboise. This is the perfect destination to experience hands-on village life in Saint-Rémy-de-Provence, and to listen to church bells chiming from the fourteenth-century bell tower of Saint-Martin while you drift off to sleep.

AT THE SAME TIME AS I DISCOVER A WORLD OUTSIDE MY FRONT DOOR I am also discovering more about my own home. A simple question that required only a straightforward answer prompted some musing on my part. When asked by my niece what was my most favourite room in the *mas*, I hesitated. I had never given this question any thought and I realised that my mind these days is focussed on external matters, on the management of the olives and on the maintenance and development of the garden, rather than the interiors.

The truth is, my home is my haven and I am mad about all of it. Of course I want to change things around, add to and rearrange my collections and reinvent spaces – I would not be a true interior junkie if I didn't – but as I made a quick mental tour of Mas de Bérard to consider my niece's question, I surprised myself. I chose our library come sitting room come television room – a place we spend time together as a family, we can take it easy with friends or I can sit for a quiet moment alone.

Why is this the one? Mostly because the library conjures up happy memories. When I look around this room I see photograph albums filled with our wedding pictures, the children's milestones and our holiday snaps. In the shelves behind the sofa are all our old school magazines – every issue of David's, the children's and mine. On top are personal journals written by Emily, Venetia and Paddy – priceless reads. Some of the children's artworks are out, as the mother in me needs the childhood reminders. And ever the sentimental soul, I have kept every painting, letter or card they have given me. The same goes for birthday cards and letters from my parents.

The books, perhaps our most beloved objects of all, are a combined collection. David is a reader of biography and autobiography, so the shelves are home to some serious thinkers, whereas I favour fiction – all sorts, good and bad. Children's stories, cookbooks, gardening books, travel guides, catalogues, magazines and well-thumbed interior-design books make up the rest. Our collection of films is an equal indulgence – my idea of perfection is a glass of red, a good film and a blazing fire. This room, one of the oldest of the *mas*, has a lower ceiling than other parts of the house, so it has a cosy feel. The bookcases, formed by hand, run floor to ceiling on three sides of the room and are more like moulded niches than shelves; it seems right that our books are the recipients of such attention to detail.

The library is furnished simply; lounging is the priority. The only furniture apart from seating is an armoire. Designed as a buffet, the eighteenth-century four-door cupboard would originally have been used to hold china, glasses and cooking utensils in a kitchen. The history of this purchase says a great deal about my husband.

L'Isle sur la Sorgue is a village about forty minutes from Saint-Rémy-de-Provence and is renowned for antique shops and a regular Sunday *brocante*. After enjoying a long lazy Sunday lunch, David and I browsed through the two-storey gallery Le Quai de la Gare. David spotted the armoire upstairs and, unbeknown to me, promptly fell in love. We discussed it a little and agreed that its original condition was lovely. I thought nothing more about it; the armoire was an enormous piece of furniture and would require a complete reshuffle at home.

A week later, without my knowledge, David went back to the gallery and bought the armoire as a surprise. He didn't measure it or worry where it might fit, nor did he guess that it would take four men to deliver it or that we would end up refurnishing our library to house it; he just knew that it was meant to be. My husband is a thoughtful, generous, impulsive and impractical man, and every time I walk down the hall towards the library and see that armoire, I love him for it.

PREVIOUS PAGE – The Salon at La Maison du Village, Saint Rémy ce Provence.
LEFT – La Suite Violette at La Maison du Village, Saint Rémy de Provence.

The views from the library, on both sides, are wonderful. A pair of double doors leads out to the terrace on the southern side. This outlook from the terrace to the Alpilles, through the garden and the olive groves, is the heartbreaker of Mas de Bérard and what we have all worked so hard to create. Looking through the windows to the northern side the canal is partially obscured by a Weeping Willow tree. On a mistral day, when I am snug inside, I watch the fine branches lashing out and I listen to the Willow's howling lament as the wind roars up through the Rhône valley. This wildness of nature makes me appreciate what is inside even more.

When I visited Mas de Bérard for the very first time I thought I had discovered 'my Provence', but now I realise that this first glimpse was nothing more than a key to the door, an *entrée* to an unfamiliar world. Choosing where we live says much about the way we want to live our lives and the things that interest us. I would like the Provence in which I live and the Provence that I have yet to discover to become 'my Provence'.

PREVIOUS PAGE – A detail of the sitting room at Mas de Bérard.
RIGHT – The library at Mas de Bérard.

27TH NOVEMBER 2007

MY PRIVATE JOURNEY INTO PROVENCE HAS BEEN ONE OF DISCOVERY. I HAVE LEARNT THAT A NEW LIFE IN A FOREIGN LAND IS NOT ONLY EXCITING, CHALLENGING AND LIFE-ALTERING, BUT MORE IMPORTANTLY IT IS A NEW BEGINNING. EMBRACING SOMETHING UNFAMILIAR MEANS THAT THE ADVENTURE NEVER ENDS, AND IT IS THE DISCOVERIES I MAKE ON THIS ADVENTURE THAT KEEP ME ASKING QUESTIONS AND SEARCHING FOR ANSWERS.

THE HARVEST

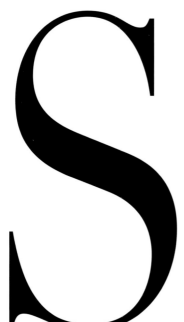

SINCE MAY THIS YEAR I have watched our olive groves with excitement and expectation: the trees, now nine years old, flowered in profusion, suggesting that the coming harvest could be the best ever.

At Mas de Bérard we have 3000 trees planted over 20 acres. The trees range in French variety, including Grossane, Salonenque and Aglandau. We follow strict farming practice outlined by the French government in order to sell our fruit to the CastelaS mill in the Vallée des Baux de Provence, which has the right to produce and sell olive oil branded as Appellation d'Origine Contrôlée (AOC).

To qualify for this prestigious label the producer must only press fruit from olive trees planted in a defined geographical area. The trees must consist of several specific varieties, be planted certain distances apart and be regularly maintained. The mill where the fruit will be pressed must be located in the production area and may only use mechanical methods to cold-extract the oil. A tasting panel must then certify the oil before it can be sold as AOC quality.

Many aspects of olive-growing sound extremely technical, but for me the most crucial element – the flowering – is romantic and somewhat mystical.

The olive trees flower for a very short time in May each year, sometimes only a week. They pollinate, then the flower dies and the fruit forms at the base of the withered flower. The more blossoms, the greater the probability that they will pollinate and bear fruit – this year our fields were on fire with creamy white promise.

Gérard, our manager, has taught me to take nothing for granted when it comes to farming. I am an optimist and he is definitely a realist – there are many temperamental elements in nature that can come into play at any time. The recipe for a successful romance and ultimate marriage between olive trees in bloom and a fruitful harvest requires a steady (but not strong) wind (definitely not the relentless mistral that is so frequent in this part of the Bouches du Rhône), no fog or heavy rain to taint or wash the flowers away, and a little bit of sunshine for good measure. Only the perfect flowers – less than 5 per cent of the whole – will bear fruit, and that is only if the weather decides to play along. It is a truly random and inexplicable selection process.

This year our farming cupid did his work – our olives blossomed, bred and bore bountiful quantities of fruit. The following months allow the fruit to settle between the leaves, and by summer I can see the olives beginning to fatten; I know that their stones will be hardening at the same time, and by August they will start to produce oil – the olives are miniscule in size but plentiful. Every evening I walk around the property with David to check their progress. Truthfully, there is very little change to witness – the fruit grow steadily and the mature olives will only become perceptible late in September – but it is not what I see but rather the promise of a full and healthy crop that piques my interest.

I have many discussions with Gérard about the forthcoming harvest. Of course he can give no definitive answers to my plague of questions because it is too early in the season, but that is not what I seek. I want to speculate about the quantity we can expect and when we might begin to pick the olives – November? Early December? Should we wait until they ripen or should we pick them when they are slightly green to ensure we lose as few as possible to winter frosts and winds? I want to know how our trees look in relation to other growers in the area and what harvesting methods will be used this year. I am relentless, like a child with too many questions and an overactive imagination. I should know better and be patient, but I cannot stop asking the questions and guessing the answers. Gérard is stoic, listening endlessly and never proffering too much opinion about what is not certain. I suspect he enjoys the conjecture as much as I do.

Autumn approaches and as the olives reach their maturity the questions become less theoretical and more practical. The bright green skins have begun to turn from mauve to aubergine as their oil content soars; by late November or early December the olives will be jet black – plump, juicy and full of oil. We must decide when to harvest: if we wait until later in the season when the oil content is higher, the tonnage will be more profitable but we risk weather conditions that could ruin our crop or at the very least cause deterioration and lessen the quantity and quality. If the temperature dips below minus three degrees at night the fruit will freeze and become bitter to the taste and impossible to press for an AOC rating.

We are again in luck: the weather holds little rain, only slight mistral winds and no sub-zero temperatures – our olives continue to ripen throughout autumn and winter.

The only misery in an otherwise textbook farming season is an unexpected attack by *les sangliers* (wild boar). While the olives prosper with high summer temperatures and minimum rainfall, the wild boar does not – their limited supply of water and food forces them out of their natural habitat. Mas de Bérard sits at the foothills of the Alpilles, and as these prehistoric-looking animals – a dozen or more – travel down from the mountains they find us easy prey. Not content to forage for food around the olive trees, where the damage would be less visible, mother, father and baby boars plough up the lawn in front of the house, rip apart the rose and iris beds and devastate the ground under the apple trees. The damage is immeasurable; pointless and heartbreaking but not unfamiliar to anyone who has spent time in southern France. I have no choice but to dry my tears, try to forgive the pigs, and imagine my garden as it will be again as I prepare for a month of hard physical labour.

We start picking the third week of November. The work is routine and the days follow the same pattern. At 7.30 each morning the tractor starts up and transports the equipment to the designated field. Gérard has assembled his team of helpers, friends and family – all men, ranging in age from twenty to sixty-plus. They are all Frenchmen but some are of Moroccan, Algerian and Tunisian background, so they speak a melange of Berber, French and Arabic – no English. There is no requisite uniform for this job, but flannel checked shirts, bottle-green overalls, colourful woollen hats, heavy boots and fat puffer jackets make up the dress code. The older men are wiry, with weathered faces that could tell a tale or two if only I could understand them. They have done this job before and waste no time starting to pick.

Underneath each olive tree a net is positioned to catch the falling fruit. There can be no gaps or holes for escapees – every olive is part of the budget. The nets are fabricated from a woven plastic mesh, rectangular and divided in half by a seam. The seam is sewn halfway and the open part wraps easily around the base of the trunks. The woven plastic is tight enough to capture the olives but open enough to allow small stones to fall through – nothing is more damaging to the mill machinery than a rogue stone.

We work in pairs, standing at opposite sides of the trees as we pick either by hand or using the long-handled combs favoured in Provence. These wooden combs are approximately 12 inches in length, with yellow plastic teeth set about half an inch apart at the base of the handle. I prefer to pick the olives by hand – I section my branches and use both hands to remove the olives in sweeping gestures. It reminds me of detangling and brushing my daughters' long hair before school.

The combs make a tapping noise as they swish through the branches. The men ply the combs through the olives tresses at great speed and then beat the remaining branches for any olives that are left. Everyone finds a pace, a partner and their own rhythm.

RIGHT – Momo with a crate of olives that are picked and ready to be sent to the Mill.
FOLLOWING PAGES – The nets draped under the olive trees.

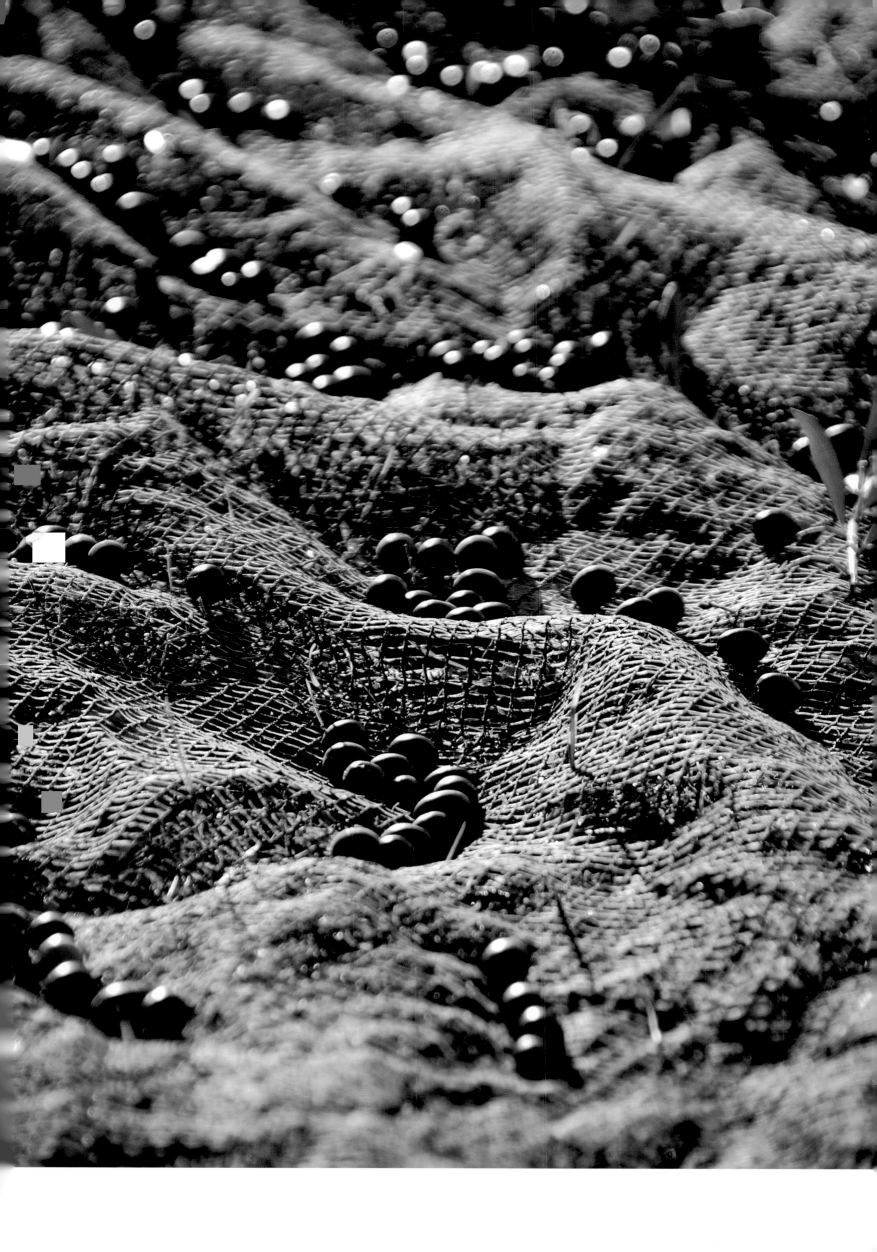

Gérard and I are a team this day. We understand each other and laugh at how little of the other men's conversations we comprehend. As we pick, I enjoy times of solitude to reflect on this unlikely place I have found myself in, and he hums Andrew Lloyd Weber show tunes – *Cats* is a favourite. The other men have chosen their partners and each couple works their routine; together, we are a strange bunch. A dance is in play up and down the rows of olives. From time to time someone cuts in and partners change, but the steps continue until 10.30, when we break for morning tea – just five minutes, so we don't lose our rhythm or succumb to the cold.

Moving from tree to tree has its own tempo. To reposition the net without losing the spoils requires precision and teamwork. One side of the net must be carefully lifted with both hands and the olives directed to the other side with a rolling motion – the slippery texture of the net facilitates this action. The olives are then gently funnelled into a case for transportation. The empty net is gathered up from one side and held close to the body. The bulk is then thrown over the arm and trails behind, forming a train. Walking between the olive trees, dripping and tripping in green mesh, I feel like a young bride juggling her veil for the bridal waltz. The net is then unrolled towards the base of the next tree and wrapped around the trunk in readiness.

The olives must be pressed within twenty-four hours of picking, and this year we make at least two trips a day to the mill with our fruit. Gérard and I always make these trips together, and we have formed a strong bond in our united goal. We are both fervent about the olives and take tremendous pride in the quantity and quality of our fruit and the progress we have made in an agricultural world previously unknown to either of us.

CastelaS mill is near the village of Les-Baux-de-Provence, about ten minutes' drive from Mas de Bérard. Situated amid breathtaking Provençal countryside, the property is surrounded by almond trees, olive trees and vineyards. Gérard and I arrive with our first load just before lunch. On receipt of the olives they must be labelled, weighed and the variety noted – olives are picked and pressed by variety and blended together afterwards. We have managed to pick three pallets of olives most days, which means a little over a tonne, so the weighing of our spoils is a wonderful highlight.

Lunch is in full swing when we arrive back at the farm. We eat together, picnic style, and share our food. It is not a long affair but it is convivial, and thankfully French is the language of choice – between the Provençal and the Moroccan accents, my understanding is hazy, but it doesn't really matter and is hardly the point. The men's exotic North African fare is warming and delicious after the long morning, and the ripe clementines that finish the meal add a tang of citrus to the air. We start again at 2 p.m. and work contentedly until the 4.30 p.m. finish. The men empty the crates and refill the pallets as Gérard and I head back to the mill.

The afternoons are the times I take pleasure in – we can spend longer at the mill as the day's picking is complete. Our car chat involves an analysis of the day's activity. Which trees have the most fruit and why? Will a certain variety have a better oil yield than others? Should we have planted more or less of a particular variety? We talk about the weather endlessly – something farmers worldwide have in common whatever language they speak. On arrival at CastelaS we muse over whether our olives are the best looking – of course I think they are and Gérard cannot wait to make the comparison. He is a perfectionist by nature and his tending, nurturing and understanding of olives has stood us in good stead.

CASTELAS MILL is owned and operated by Jean-Benoît Hugues and his wife, Catherine. Jean-Benoît describes himself as 'the American Frenchman' – he and Catherine lived and worked in the United States for fifteen years before settling back in their native Provence in 1995. They now own more than 12 000 trees and produce between 25 000 and 35 000 litres of olive oil every year, which is sold in France, throughout Europe and in the United States and has earned them the prestigious

LEFT – Loading the crates and combing the trees.
FOLLOWING PAGES – A commode in my bedroom at Mas de Bérard; the painted finish reminiscent of the colours of the harvest.

Medaille d'Or in Paris on numerous occasions. I have been working with Jean-Benoît and Catherine for several years now and am grateful that the olives from Mas de Bérard keep such prestigious company.

According to Jean-Benoît, the only place in the world where taste and expectations for olive oil differ is in Provence. French people born and bred in the south prefer over-ripe oil, a heavier, richer flavour to remind them of the olive oil of their youth. The rest of the world, without these links to the past, prefers a clean, fresh, tangy taste that comes from the highly developed pressing and extracting methods.

As our olives make their way along the conveyor belt I am content that they will be pressed in excellent conditions and used to produce some of the finest olive oil not only in France but the world. That is satisfaction indeed.

By MID DECEMBER we have picked almost 20 tonnes of olives – a record year for Mas de Bérard and almost three times as many as last year. It has been a slow process by hand with many willing helpers, and talk inevitably surfaces about mechanical harvesting. Many olive growers in Provence, including Jean-Benoît and Catherine, use electric combs to harvest their olive trees in order to reduce labour costs and meet time constraints.

This system requires a team of three – one to wear and operate the electric comb and two to lay and change the nets. A rake-like apparatus is powered and supported by a battery backpack. This vibrating rake is used to attack each branch and loosen the olives, allowing them to fall freely and be caught in the super-sized nets. One of the three workers strips the tree with the machine while the others lift, empty and replace the nets. Used effectively on plentiful trees, it probably can cut harvesting time in half. If the olive trees at Mas de Bérard continue to prosper, this inevitably will be my future. I cannot begin to imagine my harvest in this way – I will not welcome the noise of machinery in my tranquil fields.

The end of the olive harvest is a bittersweet time. Bitter, because I will miss the fun and companionship of working with friends, the camaraderie of a shared goal and the colourful differences between our cultures and languages. To labour in the outdoors is a tonic, a privilege and a freedom from everyday anxieties and pressures. I feel apprehensive that the old methods are slipping away and progress for commercial success must rule the day.

But this time is also sweet. I have celebrated a successful farming year and I am energised and full of hope for my future crops. Christmas with my husband and children is only weeks away and the magic of next May a mere five months.

RIGHT – The olive oil in final stages at CaStelas Mill.
FOLLOWING PAGE – An armoire in my bedroom at Mas de Bérard.

THE END OF THE OLIVE HARVEST IS A BITTERSWEET TIME. BITTER, BECAUSE I WILL MISS THE FUN AND COMPANIONSHIP OF WORKING WITH FRIENDS, THE CAMARADERIE OF A SHARED GOAL AND THE COLOURFUL DIFFERENCES BETWEEN OUR CULTURES AND LANGUAGES.

AVIGNON

I BELIEVE THAT ROMANCE makes the world a brighter and better place. I believe in the romance of history, the tales of battles fought and lost. I believe in the romance of architecture and the secrets concealed within. I believe in the old-fashioned, tug-at-the-heartstrings, gut-wrenching romance that makes you weep and hope at the same time. Combine a historical setting such as the Opera Theatre in Avignon with Guiseppe Verdi's epic love story *La traviata*, and there is no greater romance.

Crossing Place de l'Horloge in the walled city of Avignon, I walk amid market stalls under an open ceiling of Christmas lights on my way to the theatre. My favourite carousel in all of Provence is turning – the painted horses gallop up and down in full Belle Époque glory and the carriages twirl as they go round and round. Some of the children on the carousel swing wide off the horses and others hold on tight as if their lives depended on it. The French flag flies high above the majestic eighteenth-century town hall, and the clock tower has just sounded the hour. It is early December and preparations are well underway for the festive season. This year Avignon is celebrating Christmas as 'a city of lights' and the main boulevards, the squares, the city wall, Le Pont d' Avignon and Le Palais des Papes are shimmering.

Sculptures of the French playwrights Corneille and Molière dominate the façade of the Opera House. It seems perfect that these two dramatists are watching over the building, Corneille the master of tragedy and Molière the master of comedy. I enter the theatre, emotions braced for a roller-coaster ride of passion and tragedy, but I will leave with renewed spirits, knowing that comedy is in the wings to cheer my soul. The atmosphere in the foyer is charged as we mix together: the serious opera lovers who know every act and every aria, and the novices like me – big softies who enjoy a tale of lost love set to spine-tingling music. I find nothing so compelling as the unlikely love between a courtesan and a nobleman (think *Moulin Rouge* or the modern-day *Pretty Woman*). Opera lovers and romance lovers, we are all impatient to be immersed in the turbulent love affair between Violetta Valery and Alfredo Germont.

Larger and more important opera houses pale into insignificance alongside Avignon's precious jewel. The décor within the theatre is opulent, like a more sophisticated version of the circus tent in Perpingnan: red velvet and fringing, tassels aplenty and beautifully ornate balconies. The atmosphere is intimate; I feel wrapped up and cosseted for the performance.

The lights dim and the buzz of our chatter fades as the orchestra strikes up. The curtain rises on Violetta's salon in Paris: a party is in progress to celebrate her return to health after a long illness. The courtesan Violetta is introduced to Alfredo, the nobleman who has been deeply devoted to her during her illness, and now declares his love for her. In this instant every woman in the theatre falls in love with Alfredo, and we inch forward on our seats as we wait for Violetta's response. This is a moment when a heart is laid open with such vulnerability and the knowledge that rejection is possible. Alfredo is the ultimate brave and sincere gentleman – the kind of man we women dream of. Violetta is

initially reluctant to accept his attentions but she finds something compelling in Alfredo's innocence and truthfulness and agrees to meet him again.

A romance is born and three months later Alfredo and Violetta are living together in the countryside outside of Paris. Violetta has renounced her former life as a courtesan and fallen completely in love with Alfredo. This is where I (and I suspect all the other romantics in the theatre) want the story to end, on a note of happiness, of romance and long-lasting love, but tonight happily ever after is not to be.

Unbeknown to Alfredo, his father visits Violetta and begs her to end the relationship for the sake of his family's reputation. Deep in our hearts we hope that Violetta will defy him, but she is a nobler creature than her audience, so she agrees to give up Alfredo for the sake of his family. Violetta departs for Paris, leaving Alfredo a parting letter telling him only that their affair is over. Alfredo is devastated.

The audience seethes; the mood in the theatre is tense. I feel as if Alfredo and Violetta are singing only to me and that their pain is my pain. Looking across the balcony, I see I am not the only one enthralled.

Alfredo rushes back to Paris to confront Violetta. Blind to her unfaltering love, the sight of her with another man at a party sends Alfredo into a rage and straight for the gaming tables. Love and jealousy are dangerous partners; in temper, he throws his winnings at her feet and announces they are payment for her services during the time they spent together. Shocked and disgusted by his behaviour, Violetta's companion challenges Alfredo to a duel. Both men survive the duel, but the lovers' quarrel and separation wastes precious time. Six months pass before Alfredo learns of his father's hand in his heartbreak. Alfredo rushes to Violetta's side to beg her forgiveness. Tragically he is too late: her tuberculosis is critical and the doctor cannot save her. Their idyllic life together can be one of only moments. Violetta acknowledges Alfredo's pain and torment, accepts his infinite love and dies reconciled in his arms.

There is not a dry eye in the theatre. I think we are shedding tears not only for Violetta and Alfredo, but for the memories of our own broken hearts – there is a little bit of lost and torturous love in all of us tonight. However short-lived is this *grand amour*, the romantics among us are content; it is not the length of the love affair that is important but the depth of the feelings. Real romance is the knowledge and experience of profound love.

L E PALAIS DES PAPES AND LE PONT D'AVIGNON (also known as Le Pont Saint Bénezet) are for me the romantic symbols of Avignon. The palace is one of the largest Gothic buildings in Europe, built alongside the Notre-Dame des Doms cathedral; together they dominate the skyline of the medieval city.

Le Pont d'Avignon was made famous by the French song '*Sur le pont d'Avignon*'. I learnt this song at school and cannot help but hum the chorus when I pass beside the bridge on my way in and out of the walled city.

Sur le pont d'Avignon
On y danse, on y danse
Sur le pont d'Avignon
On y danse tout en rond

On the bridge of Avignon
We dance, we dance,
On the bridge of Avignon
We dance around in a ring

PREVIOUS PAGES – A cobblestone street beside the Palais des Papes.
A corner of the sitting room at Mas de Bérard.
RIGHT – Detail of an engraving in my bedroom.

Built between 1175 and 1185, the bridge was repaired and restored over the centuries until 1668 when the majority of it collapsed during a monumental flooding. The bridge is not so much for dancing these days, as only four arches remain of the original twenty-two that once crossed the Rhône River and connected Avignon with the village of Villeneuve-lès-Avignon. The view from the top of this village, across the river, is the best vantage point from which to appreciate Le Pont d'Avignon, Notre Dame des Dom and Le Palais des Papes.

It is the story of how the bridge came to be that makes me smile. A local shepherd boy, Saint Bénézet, claimed that angels appeared to him in a dream and told him to build a bridge across the Rhône. His dream was dismissed as nonsense until, by some miracle, he single-handedly lifted a massive block of stone – an impossible feat for any one person. Saint Bénézet became a hero overnight and funds were found to build his 'dream' bridge. He is buried in the small chapel above one of the remaining piers, and I like to think he and his angels watch over all who enter the great city walls of Avignon.

In July and August the walkways along the Rhône River (and most of the town walls) are covered with posters celebrating the Festival d'Avignon. These clever cardboards add a riot of colour to the medieval city and advertise the theatrical events taking place each evening. The festival supports contemporary dance and dramatic productions from French and international performers in more than twenty different venues around the city, including Le Palais des Papes, churches and schools.

The medieval wall and gateways that enclose the old city of Avignon are a legacy from the papal era. The wall, built between 1349 and 1368, was never intended as a serious determent for villains but more as an imposing entry to the city and the papal palace. Le Palais des Papes was home to the Catholic papacy for most of the fourteenth century, when the papacy left Rome in search of political stability. In exchange they provided Avignon with a long period of peaceful government, financial prosperity and cultural refinement. Although the papacy returned to Rome in 1377, Avignon continued to be governed by the Papal Legate until the French Revolution in 1789. Once behind these massive walls I too feel protected and calmed by the popes' intangible presence.

AVIGNON IS THE HOME OF DISCRETION, a city of secret entrances and hidden courtyards. Beneath Le Palais des Papes the cobbled streets lead to Place de La Mirande and a pair of nondescript wooden doors: behind these doors is a family-run hotel with a history that dates back to the fourteenth century. Cardinal Pellegrue, a nephew of Avignon's first pope, Clement V, built the property in 1309 to hold receptions for the pope, his cardinals and visiting guests. Over the centuries the building changed hands and purposes, until the present owners discovered it in 1987; they changed the name to La Mirande and devoted three years to restoring the hotel into the handsome residence it is today. A quiet, calm haven from the noise, activity and crowds of this popular city, La Mirande embodies old-style European grace. Like the Opera Theatre in the Place de l'Horloge, La Mirande is a living, breathing historical monument; the very act of being here makes one feel a part of the history of Avignon. Whether resting weary feet after a visit to the palace, enjoying an *apéritif* before the opera or partaking in an overnight romantic tryst, a visit to La Mirande is heaven.

The visual success of La Mirande is the result of a passionate collaboration between owners Achim and Hannelore Stein, Parisian interior designer François-Joseph Graf and Avignon architect Gilles Grégoire. Between them they have merged eighteenth- and nineteenth-century decorating styles and created the impression of a private home. La Mirande is very French but manages not to intimidate. My every visit to La Mirande sparks a desire to redecorate or rearrange some part of Mas de Bérard. The soft furnishings, the paintings, the china collections and the antique furniture at La Mirande are the template for my 'interiors' wish list.

The light-filled inner courtyard is the heart of the hotel and is the ideal place to watch the comings and goings of a hotel in action. Rattan tables and chairs are informally arranged around

PREVIOUS PAGE – The Palais des Papes, looking back from Villeneuve-lès-Avignon.
LEFT – Posters from the Avignon Festival.
FOLLOWING PAGES – The bar and a detail of the chandelier at La Mirande, Avignon.

a central pinewood table. This long trestle-style table holds bowls of fruit, or cakes and sandwiches in the late afternoon. The latest magazines, big 'flick' books and the newspapers are available to inform and amuse.

A curved stone staircase leads to the upstairs bedrooms, and narrow corridors run off towards the more formal parts of La Mirande. The breakfast room, painted ballerina pink, is named Le Salon Jardin for the perspective it has over the garden courtyard. The small salon cum reading room next door is Le Cabinet Chinois, named for the hand-painted eighteenth-century Chinese wallpaper; this room is exquisite in every way – a view of Le Palais des Papes, a desk at which to write letters, a squishy oversized armchair in which to disappear or just to gaze at the colourful peacocks and nightingales on the wallpaper is pleasure enough for me.

Another opening off the courtyard leads to the bar and Le Salon Rouge. Both rooms are charismatic, the kind I want to slink and sink in. The bar is all about the oversized chandelier and the blue-grey woodwork; the red salon is pure glamour and romance. Bold striped wallpaper, Jacquard-print fabrics, heavy fringing, a million buttons plus candles and wall lights – Le Salon Rouge is ambience Avignon style.

The main dining room, La Salle Cardinalice, is simply furnished, except for a wonderful seventeenth-century Brussels tapestry. If the weather unexpectedly fails, lunch in this gorgeous room is another way to experience the delights of the city of popes: a glass of champagne, the mouth-watering tastes of the market menu, and unsurprisingly, two hours later sightseeing seems effortless.

Small spiral stairs sneak down to the original nineteenth-century kitchen. This room has been retained as a secondary workspace for guests to enjoy communal dinners or host private parties. The kitchen is complete with copper pans, wood-fired oven, earthenware plates and other old-fashioned equipment rarely seen in commercial facilities today. This room is also where the La Marmiton cooking classes take place, during which participants sit around a vast central table and listen, learn and eat as celebrated chefs from the region instruct in the ways of Provençal fare and French cuisine.

The decorative beauty of La Mirande is in the attention to detail. The paintings are from the owner's personal collection and are hung with great care and consideration for their surroundings. The interaction between the painting and the position it holds in each room is as important as the frame that holds the work or the artist that painted it.

The fabrics that cover the furniture and walls at La Mirande have been meticulously researched. Some of the bedrooms are lined with cotton document prints originally fabricated by the royal manufacturer at Jouy, near Versailles. These new prints are authentic because they reproduce the same patterns as those printed at Jouy and are simply additions to an existing series. These exotic depictions of travel and adventure became the mode in the eighteenth century and were best known as 'chinoiserie' – a blend of English and Chinese images representing travel, romantic love and nature. These faithful re-creations have given the hotel an age-of-enlightenment spirit and afford a glimpse into the past.

La Mirande is a setting in which I can easily imagine Alfredo and Violetta living the fairytale ending, protected by the spiritual presence of Le Palais des Papes and watched over by Saint Bénézet from Le Pont d'Avignon.

The Avignon I love is less about visiting the guidebook hot spots and more about soaking up the ambience and revelling in the romance of living history. An encounter with Avignon is an elegant pause from our modern world and a window through which to view the grandeur of an old-style Europe.

THE PAINTINGS ARE FROM THE OWNER'S PERSONAL
COLLECTION AND ARE HUNG WITH GREAT CARE
AND CONSIDERATION FOR THEIR SURROUNDINGS.
THE INTERACTION BETWEEN THE PAINTING AND THE
POSITION IT HOLDS IN EACH ROOM IS AS IMPORTANT
AS THE FRAME THAT HOLDS THE WORK OR THE ARTIST
THAT PAINTED IT.

CHRISTMAS

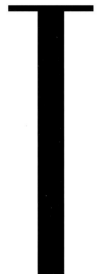

IT IS SNOWING. Snow is rare in my part of Provence and only falls every three or four years. It is not a surprise this particular morning, however; there have been signs. The temperature in early December has been dropping and while sunny and clear, has often been little above zero. Yesterday blue skies gave way to an even mass of cloud that gradually settled over Mas de Bérard. The temperature dipped below minus-four last night and the cloud stayed low.

This morning the dormant sky had vanished. The smooth cloud of yesterday was replaced by an indigo blue, almost black, bulk gathering momentum and closing us in. Outside it was silent. That is the strange thing before a snowfall: it is deadly quiet, as if Mother Nature is holding her breath until the first flake falls.

And then it happened. The snow fell gently and quickly. Perfectly formed flakes masked our bare winter landscape. The clipped green topiaries, the amphitheatre of dried lavender and the garden hedges seemed to snatch the snow first. As the lawn transformed into a white wonderland and the ground between the fruit and olive trees vanished, so too did the *sanglier* debacle. Everything is renewed, fresh and sparkling – an auspicious start to the Christmas season.

Christmas is a close family time for us, and I have always taken pleasure in dressing our home and continuing the traditions that I learnt as a child. The trimming of the tree and the other embellishments of this holiday are not a drudge – I relish every moment spent planning and find great pleasure in creating the ambience that my family has grown to love. Living in France has not changed my approach; I have simply added a Provençal dimension to our celebrations.

A sweeping staircase dominates our entrance hall at Mas de Bérard. A sparse and voluminous space, it is a wonderful 'room' to create impact and in which to follow the Provençal habit of using the olive branch as a form of decoration. This year I have attached and covered the iron balustrade with the largest branches and bound the smaller twigs around the railing. The leaves have shaped themselves into a thick barrier and curve upwards from the bottom step to the top landing. Each evening I line the stone stairs with glass beakers; the tea lights within flicker to cast shadows against the walls. The olive tree is an ancient symbol of peace and wisdom, and the unruly branches make a fitting backdrop for our Christmas tree.

Trimming the tree is the most fun. This year I have chosen a theme of red, lime green and purple. Traditionally David and I put the tree in place and position the fairy lights, and Emily, Venetia and Paddy take care of the rest. It has always been this way and is a time for me to bite my words and be content with their decorative decision-making. Anyone who is as painfully fussy as I am knows that this is tough stuff.

PREVIOUS PAGE – Mas de Bérard in snow.
LEFT – The 'olive garland' staircase.

LEFT AND RIGHT – Venetia trimming the tree.

When I decorate, I like to build the ornaments up in layers. The first step is to hang the many red balls; painted to look like velvet damask, they are placed halfway along each of the branches and evenly distributed over the tree. Violet comes next. These balls are smaller, made of silvery glass, and sit snugly in the fork of the limbs. Our tree is taking shape; the richness of the red and purple contrasts with the deep green, and the twinkling lights play well with the reflective surfaces of the decorations.

Our special ornaments are the sentimental and most precious ones. I have been collecting Christmas decorations for decades and each one can remind me of a particular year, a specific holiday or just a flash memory of one of the children. Every Christmas since they were born I have bought them a new ornament. As they grew up they loved to choose their own. We always made a day of it – a visit to Santa, the obligatory photograph and a new bauble.

The most beautiful ones tend to be the storybook characters. We have hand-painted Santas and wand-carrying Merlins, Bambi, Snow White and her Prince. We have snowmen and gingerbread men, gold-winged angels and magical fairies, sequined fish and beaded monkeys, felt kangaroos, nightingales and robins, plums and apricots – even peas and carrots. Then there is the train carriage and the New York taxi, the lighthouse from the French comic *Tintin* and the sugared house from Hansel and Gretel. Each one is unique and exquisite.

Now that these prized trinkets are in place, the only outstanding feature is the angel: we will place her on top, cover the tree with fine tinsel and wrap the presents.

I love to fuss with my presents, and I believe it is as important to spend the time wrapping them as it is to choose them – the anticipation of what is inside those pretty packages is what the excitement is all about.

My wrapping is bold this year. I am following the theme of red, lime green and purple to include matching tissue paper, ribbon and feathers. Into the paper mix I add some French newspapers, *Le Monde* and *La Provence*. The ribbons are grosgrain and silk satin, and the feathers are plain dyed chicken-yard variety. Colour on colour and texture on texture – red tissue, red grosgrain and red feathers look quirky contrasted against newspaper-clad parcels tied with silk satin and finished with multiple feathers.

The mantra, 'Those who don't believe, don't receive' is alive and well in our household: we all believe in Santa and that is that. Santa arrives by sleigh on Christmas Eve, squeezes down the chimney and is fortified by a small shot of whiskey while he sorts the loot. The only hint that he is *Papa Noël* rather than Father Christmas is the basket of goodies he leaves instead of the stuffed pillowcases. A woven basket is waiting by the hearth for Santa to fill and deliver to the foot of each bed ready for Christmas morning. As a nod to our French Father Christmas not only are these baskets filled with gifts but also sweets, nuts and fruit.

A**S I MAKE MY PREPARATIONS**, the villagers of Saint-Rémy-de-Provence hang their Christmas lights and build the small wooden cabins that will house the Christmas market. Whether in a larger town or city like Avignon or a small village like mine, the French are maestros when it comes to Christmas lights.

The village looks like a fairyland. Around the circumference residents and holidaymakers are welcomed with illuminated banners that wish *Joyeuses Fêtes* (Happy Holidays) and *Joyeux Noël* (Merry Christmas). Garlands of small lights brighten the pathways that lead to the town square, bordered on one side by the impressive town hall. This square is cornered by large plane trees, cascading with tiny lights, and centred with a fountain. Above the plane trees strings of fairy lights form a circus-style canopy. Against the night sky, the square appears brilliant, as if dressed with diamonds. Suspended from the apex of the canopy are sparkling spheres of blue, white and red – a patriotic tribute floating in a starry firmament.

RIGHT – The library, Mas de Bérard.
FOLLOWING PAGE – Fairy lights at the Town Hall.

LEFT – Amaryllis and the decorated chandelier.
RIGHT – A detail of the table setting and a collection of red baubles.

The Christmas market is a French tradition, and ours in Saint-Rémy-de-Provence is held the weekend before Christmas. An organ-grinder winds out 'Jingle Bells' and some children clap and sing along to the tune. The words they sing have nothing to do with jingling bells and a horse-drawn sleigh but rather they are singing an ode to the wind:

Vive le vent, vive le vent
Vive le vent d'hiver
Qui s'en va sifflant, soufflant
Dans les grands sapins verts
Oh!
Vive le vent, vive le vent
Vive le temps d'hiver
Boule de neige et jour de l'an
Et bonne année grand-mère

Translated, they are singing:

Live the wind, live the wind
Live the winter wind
Which goes whistling, blowing
In the big green fir trees
Oh!
Live the wind, live the wind
Live the winter weather
Snowball and New Year's Day
And Happy New Year, Grandmother

Their little voices sound sweet and the words are apt in the chilling wind and freezing temperature of this December afternoon. A woman is roasting chestnuts in a pan over an open fire and the smell is irresistible. They are served piping hot in a twist of newspaper. There is something about the smell of roasting chestnuts and the quirky sound of organ music that feels so European and for me is still such a novelty.

Several market stands are devoted to *les santons*, the clay figurines depicting local characters that are a well-loved traditional symbol of Christmas in Provence. The word *santon* comes from the old Provençal vernacular *santoun* meaning 'little saint'. These figurines first became popular during the French Revolution when public nativity scenes were prohibited and the churches closed; as a result, small replicas were manufactured that could be assembled at home. Taking up this idea, *les santons* first appeared at a Christmas fair in Marseille in 1803, from which a local legend was born. Skilled artisans produced figurines that not only represented the nativity scene but also characters of the village, such as the butcher, the baker, the mayor, the cafe owner, the shepherd, the farmer and his wife. According to the legend, Jesus was born in Provence and the crèche represents the village at the time of his birth. Last night in Saint-Rémy the villagers enacted this story in Place Favier, outside the Musée des Alpilles. The angel Gabriel, perched high in a plane tree, narrated the tale and the local acting troop mimed the roles. This Provençal twist on the story of Christmas is lovely – full of high drama and romance.

Food dominates the other stalls in the market. Dried and glacé fruit, compotes and jams, all sorts of nuts – almonds, cashews pistachios and peanuts, salted and plain – are being weighed and bought for the Christmas feast. There are fruitcakes and biscuits from the local *boulangeries*, nougats from Montpellier and *calissons* from Aix-en-Provence. Vendors offer trays of *fougasse*, a sweet or savoury

RIGHT – Sylvain.
FOLLOWING PAGE – Favourite decorations.

216

plaited bread that can be filled with dried figs and nuts, olives, cheese or bacon; the loaves are either dusted in fine sugar or sprinkled with olive oil.

There are balsamic vinegars, olive oils and fresh herbs, and pots of *fleur de sel* – the thick flaky sea salt hand-harvested in the Camargue – are arranged in a pyramid. The duck or goose *foie gras* is available in tins, hessian bags or porcelain tubs. Wine vendors open bottles: red, white, champagne and sauterne are offered for tasting. Most French outings revolve around a happy digestion, and the Christmas market is no exception – there is a bar serving ice-cold champagne and freshly shucked oysters.

These delectable goods are all bought to celebrate *le réveillon* (the midnight supper), a feast that begins on Christmas Eve before the midnight mass service. The feast is generally made up of seven main dishes, to symbolise the seven sorrows of Mary. The meal will begin with a soup dish, followed by fish, turkey, game or chicken and a selection of vegetables. Guests will then be offered *les treize desserts* (thirteen desserts), which represent Christ and his twelve disciples. These desserts include sweets, fresh and dried fruits, nuts, cakes, biscuits and breads, and it is customary for all at the table to taste each of the thirteen desserts.

Traditional cakes are served throughout the French holiday season. La bûche de Noël is a log-shaped cake made of chocolate and chestnuts to represent the special fruitwood burned from Christmas Eve to New Year's Day. These logs are iced with a creamy frosting and decorated with small scenes of country life – the skier, the snowman or the hunter in the forest. La galette des Rois, a brioche sprinkled with crystallised fruit, is baked with a lucky charm inside and topped with a paper crown. This cake celebrates the Epiphany or Three Kings Day at the end of the advent season – the twelfth day of Christmas. The galette is sliced like a pie, and the person who finds the charm in their slice wears the paper crown.

AT HOME I AM PLANNING FOR OUR FEAST. I have covered the dining table with a red velvet *boutis*, the Provençal-style quilt used for everything from bedspreads and tablecloths to outdoor picnic rugs. I was given some monogrammed linen napkins in October, and the red-embroidered 'A' sits well against the velvet, so I place one in the centre of each plate. Red champagne and water glasses mix prettily with the crystal wine goblets. Some rose, red and silver miniature baubles, sprinkled over the table, will serve as place cards: I will write our names with gold and silver markers on the larger ones and place them in the centre of the napkins with the bonbons before we sit down on Christmas Day.

Three mercury-glass fir trees form the centrepiece of my table beneath a wooden chandelier. This old Provençal light has a faded patina. Made up of six carved arms supporting two candle bulbs each, it is suspended on a heavy chain from the ceiling. Underneath each light I secure a red and gold ornament with a length of fishing line; simple bows of gold organza hide my attachments. I wind the chain with the same ribbon and place small lampshades – made from two different shades of red linen – over the bulbs. This handsomely dressed chandelier glitters both when the sun streams through the glass doors and when there is only candlelight and firelight to light the room. Dressing the chandelier adds another dimension to our dining room. This whimsical creation of organza, glitter and red glass has transformed and softened a simple space that is normally dominated by a Chinese cultural poster from Mao days, a stone fireplace and a French draper's armoire.

I will finish decorating the Christmas table with a pair of tall rectangular vases: in each I will place four blood-red stems of amaryllis. Red tulips will adorn the armoire. When I visit Emmanuelle and Sylvain at Le Bouquet aux Jules florist in the village to collect my flowers, Sylvain asks if I have ever seen *le gui* (mistletoe). In Provence mistletoe grows mainly in oak trees and forms an almost perfectly round mass in the crown of the tree. At Christmas it is the female plants – covered with waxy white berries – that are used for decoration. Sylvain explains that hanging mistletoe at home wishes good

LEFT – The Christmas table.
FOLLOWING PAGE – A commode in the dining room at Mas de Bérard.

221

health, happiness and fortune for the coming year. I know of the 'kissing under the mistletoe' tradition but this is the first time I have seen the plant close up. Driving through Provence in the winter, I have seen the mysterious silhouettes in the bare trees and not realised their beauty or their meaning.

I like to believe the Gallic legend that tells of King Gwyder and his three betrothed daughters. The men, leaving for war, farewell the girls under the ancient oak trees heavy with mistletoe. The men demand a memento, so the girls give them a peacock feather from their hair; the men demand another, so the girls give the small sprigs of holly that held the feathers in place; not content, the men ask for something more: the girls have nothing else to give, so they offer a kiss – a kiss under the mistletoe.

AS A CHILD I ALWAYS LOOKED FORWARD TO CHRISTMAS LUNCH: roast turkey with all the accompaniments, and the plum pudding and brandy butter made by my mother. Although I now celebrate Christmas in the French way, it is never without plum pudding. This dessert may not be part of the French food tradition, but the turkey certainly is. The French love their Christmas turkey, and in the month before Christmas they hold food markets, festivals and fairs all over the country to showcase and sell these fowls.

In France, the Christmas turkey cannot be just any turkey, though. Leaving aside whether they are free-range or corn-fed, the importance of provenance or whether they deserve an AOC rating, it is the question of gender that really confuses me. Does a female turkey taste any different from a male turkey? Should I roast only the mature female birds or should I play it safe and select the young, innocent female? I don't even want to think about the poor emasculated adolescent male.

Over the years I have built a rapport with Monsieur Charles at my *boucherie*. He is amused by my ignorance in these matters but takes my education seriously. According to him, the choice of turkey is simply a question of personal taste. To select my fowl he must ask some questions – I have become expert at these long conversations where nothing serious hinges on the outcome, and I am happy to play along. Do I prefer the white meat or the brown meat? What texture of meat do I enjoy? How many people will the turkey need to feed? I am not sure what all this has to do with the age and sex of the bird, but I answer his questions and he chooses the turkey – a hen of indeterminate age. (I think that means not young, but he is too diplomatic to say.) He plucks the feathers, cleans and fills the cavity with a stuffing of dried apricot, sage and breadcrumbs, then weighs the bird and calculates the cooking time. He promises the meat will be tender and succulent if I follow his instructions, and he assures me that the gender and age of the turkey will ensure the flavour. Monsieur Charles is right: our turkey is a triumph.

EMILY, VENETIA AND PADDY are throwing a party to celebrate the New Year, or *le réveillon de la Sainte-Sylvestre* as the French call New Year's Eve. The invitations have stipulated the theme of the evening and the costume: the characters must hail from a fairytale, nursery rhyme or classical legend.

As Paddy sets off a fireworks display to bring in the New Year I reflect on the year that has passed. I am lucky in love, blessed with beautiful children and fortunate to be fit and healthy, so I resolve to enjoy this charmed life and to welcome the challenges, whatever they may be, that will face me in the coming year. The final rocket is launched and shoots upward, whistling high into the night sky and all but disappearing out of sight. A silence follows and then a sharp burst of sound. A lacework of fractured light erupts overhead and bathes Mas de Bérard in a rosy glow.

That is how I see it anyway.

RIGHT – Paddy.
FOLLOWING PAGE – The guest bedroom at Mas de Bérard.

I LOVE TO FUSS WITH MY PRESENTS, AND I BELIEVE IT IS AS IMPORTANT TO SPEND THE TIME WRAPPING THEM AS IT IS TO CHOOSE THEM – THE ANTICIPATION OF WHAT IS INSIDE THOSE PRETTY PACKAGES IS WHAT THE EXCITEMENT IS ALL ABOUT.

MY ADDRESS BOOK

AIX-EN-PROVENCE

Festival of Aix-en-Provence
11 Rue Gaston de Saporta
13100 Aix-en-Provence
+33 4 42 17 34 34
festival-aix.com

Office de Tourisme
2 Place Général de Gaulle
13100 Aix-en-Provence
+33 4 42 16 11 61
aixenprovencetourism.com

MUSEUMS & GALLERIES

Atelier Paul Cézanne
9 Avenue Paul Cézanne
13090 Aix-en-Provence
+33 4 42 21 06 53
atelier-cezanne.com

Fondation Vasarely
1 Avenue Marcel Pagnol
13090 Aix-en-Provence
+33 4 42 20 01 09
fondationvasarely.fr

Musée des Tapisseries
28 Place des Martyrs de la Résistance
13100 Aix-en-Provence
+33 4 42 23 09 91

Musée du Vieil Aix
17 Rue Gaston de Saporta
13100 Aix-en-Provence
+33 4 42 21 43 55

Musée Granet
Place Saint Jean de Malte
13100 Aix-en-Provence
+33 4 42 52 88 32
museegranet-aixenprovence.fr

Musée Paul Arbaud
2 Rue du 4 Septembre
13100 Aix-en-Provence
+33 4 42 38 38 95

Museum d'Histoire Naturelle
6 Rue Espariat
13100 Aix-en-Provence
+33 4 42 27 91 27
museum-aix-en-provence.org

ANTIQUES

Brocante du Cours Sextius
100 Cours Sextius
13100 Aix-en-Provence
+33 4 42 27 64 92

Brocantes de la Petite Calade
RN7 – La Petite Calade
13100 Aix-en-Provence
+33 4 42 28 30 91

Didascalies
18 Rue Fernand Dol
13100 Aix-en-Provence
+33 4 42 27 22 34
didascalies.net

Galerie Franck Marcelin
7 Rue Jaubert
13100 Aix-en-Provence
+33 4 42 23 17 38

Galerie Portalis
28 Rue Fortalis
13100 Aix-en-Provence
+33 4 42 93 20 66

Les Marches du Palais
1 Rue Chastel
13100 Aix-en-Provence
+33 4 42 38 06 55

Mazarin Antiques
8 Rue Fréderic Mistral
13100 Aix-en-Provence
+33 4 42 27 16 03

Padovani Antiques
62 Place Richelme
13100 Aix-en-Provence
+33 4 42 99 37 78

Les Paris d'Helene
4 Rue Jaubert
13100 Aix-en-Provence
+33 4 42 21 16 83

La Rotonde
2 Avenue des Belges
13100 Aix-en-Provence
+33 4 42 26 78 92

Le Village des Antiquaires
6110 Route d'Avignon
13090 Aix-en-Provence
+ 33 4 42 92 50 03

HOMEWARES & GIFTS

Carré Blanc and Descamps
55 Cours Mirabeau
13100 Aix-en-Provence
+33 4 42 27 49 29

Côté Bastide
Rue Pierre Simon Laplace
13100 Aix-en-Provence
+33 4 42 97 31 00
cotebastide.com

Décalé
14 Rue d'Italie
13100 Aix-en-Provence
+33 4 42 53 32 65

LEFT - The Carousel in the Place de l'Horloge, Avignon.

L'Esprit Demeure
57 Rue Espariat
13100 Aix-en-Provence
+33 4 42 27 87 49

L'Esprit des Lieux en Provence
10 Rue Gaston de Saporta
13100 Aix-en-Provence
+33 4 42 21 20 74

Librairie Goulard
37 Cours Mirabeau
* And 7 & 9 Rue Papassaudi
13100 Aix-en-Provence
+33 4 42 27 66 47
librairiegoulard.com

Librairie Papeterie-Aixoise
2 Rue Vauvenargues
13100 Aix-en-Provence
+33 4 42 23 31 32

La Maison 24 Saporta
24 Rue Gaston de Saporta
13100 Aix-en-Provence
+33 4 42 99 24 19
24Saporta.com

La Maison d'Hortense
35 Rue d'Italie
13100 Aix-en-Provence
+33 4 42 61 08 22

Le Nain Rouge
47 Rue Espariat
13100 Aix-en-Provence
+33 4 42 93 50 05

Sephora Aix-en-Provence
12 Rue Fabrot
13100 Aix-en-Provence
+ 33 4 42 26 74 78

Sephora Mirabeau
Avenue Napoléon-Bonaparte
13100 Aix-en-Provence
+33 4 42 61 24 60

Yves Delorme
6 Rue Ancienne Madeleine
13100 Aix-en-Provence
+33 4 42 27 00 57

FASHION

Agnés B
2 Rue Fernand Dol
13100 Aix-en-Provence
+33 4 42 38 44 87

Antoine et Lili
4 Rue Matheron
13100 Aix-en-Provence
+33 4 42 23 25 42
antoineetlili.com/

Aubade
12 Rue de Nazareth
13100 Aix-en-Provence
+33 4 42 60 09 34
aubade.com

Carlotta
9 Rue de la Glacière
13100 Aix-en-Provence
+33 4 42 26 68 50

Daniel Cremieux
9 Rue Marius Reinaud
13100 Aix-en-Provence
+33 4 42 27 44 09
danielcremieux.com

First
7 Rue Fabrot
13100 Aix-en-Provence
+33 4 42 38 51 05

Gago
20 Rue Fabrot
13100 Aix-en-Provence
+33 4 42 26 08 52

La Grande Boutique
7 Rue de la Glacière
13100 Aix-en-Provence
+33 4 42 26 30 72

Longchamp
22 Cours Mirabeau
13100 Aix-en-Provence
+33 4 42 91 52 05
longchamp.fr

Madone
14 Rue de Nazareth
13100 Aix-en-Provence
+33 4 42 27 97 18

Princesse Tam-Tam
39 Rue Espariat
13100 Aix-en-Provence
+33 4 42 38 55 16
princessetamtam.com

Scratch
32 Cours Mirabeau
13100 Aix-en-Provence
+ 33 4 42 38 00 13

Signature
34 Rue Espariat
13100 Aix-en-Provence
+33 4 42 26 29 85

Wolford
7 Rue de Nazareth
13100 Aix-en-Provence
+33 4 42 26 24 10

Zadig et Voltaire
11 Rue Marius Reinhaud
13100 Aix-en-Provence
+33 4 42 38 65 08
zadig-et-voltaire.com

FOOD & WINE

Carton Rouge
Cave Bistro à Vins
7 Rue Isolette
13100 Aix-en-Provence
+33 4 42 91 41 75

Les Calissons du Roy René
13 Rue Gaston de Saporta
13100 Aix-en-Provence
+33 4 42 26 67 86
calisson.com

La Cave des Domaines
53 Avenue Malacrida
13100 Aix-en-Provence
+33 4 42 93 53 78

La Cave d'Yves
8 Rue Portalis
13100 Aix-en-Provence
+33 4 42 93 75 80
lacavedyves.com

La Corse en Provence
7 Rue Maréchal Foch
13100 Aix-en-Provence
+33 4 42 26 38 59

La Cure Gourmande
16 Rue Vauvenargues
13100 Aix-En-Provence
+33 4 42 21 26 48
cure-gourmande.com

Chocolaterie de Puyricard
7 Rue Rifle-Rafle
13100 Aix-en-Provence
+33 4 42 21 13 26

Comtesse du Barry
55 Rue Espariat
13100 Aix-en-Provence
+33 4 42 27 04 24
comtessedubarry.com

Les Deux Garçons
53 Cours Mirabeau
13100 Aix-en-Provence
+33 4 42 26 00 51

La Fournée de Joseph
32 Rue Portalis
13100 Aix-en-Provence
+33 4 42 29 62 80

Geisha Sushi Experience
53 Cours Mirabeau
13100 Aix-en-Provence
+33 4 42 20 30 00
sushi-geisha.com

Hediard
18 Rue d'Italie
13100 Aix-en-Provence
+33 4 42 61 52 58
hediard.fr

Jacquèmes
9 Rue Méjanes
13100 Aix-en-Provence
+33 4 42 23 48 64
jacquemes.fr

Le Marché des Chefs
7 Place Miollis
13100 Aix-en-Provence
+33 4 42 38 97 38

Place aux Huiles
59 Rue d'Italie
13100 Aix-en-Provence
+33 4 42 38 71 77

Place aux Huiles
14 Rue Gaston de Saporta
13100 Aix-en-Provence
+33 4 42 96 21 28

CINEMAS

Le Cezanne
1 Rue Marcel Guillaume
13100 Aix-en-Provence
+33 8 92 63 72 70

Le Mazarin
6 Rue Laroque
13100 Aix-en-Provence
+33 4 42 26 61 51

Le Renoir
24 Cours Mirabeau
13100 Aix-en-Provence
+33 8 36 68 72 70

MARKETS

Marché Brocante Antiquités
Second Sunday of every month
Cours Mirabeau
Place de Verdun
Tuesday, Thursday and Saturday

Marché aux livres anciens
First Sunday of every month
Place de l'Hôtel-de-Ville

Marché Paysan
Tuesday, Thursday and Saturday
Centre Ville

AVIGNON

Festival of Avignon
Bureau du Festival d'Avignon
(Programs and tickets)
Cloitre Saint Louis
20 Rue du Portail Boquier
84000 Avignon
+33 4 90 27 66 50
festival-avignon.com

Office de tourisme
41 Cours Jean Jaurès
84000 Avignon
+33 4 32 74 32 74
ot-avignon.fr

Opera Theatre Avignon
Plade d'Horloge
84000 Avignon
+33 4 90 82 42 42
operatheatredavignon.fr

Le Palais des Papes
Place du Palais des Papes
84000 Avignon
+33 4 90 27 50 00
palais-des-papes.com

Le Pont Saint Bénezet
Rue Ferruce
84000 Avignon
+33 4 90 27 51 16

MUSEUMS & GALLERIES

La Collection Lambert
5 Rue Viclette
84000 Avignon
+33 4 90 16 56 20
collectionlambert.com

Maison Jean Vilar
8 Rue de Mons
84000 Avignon
+33 4 90 86 59 64
maisonjeanvilar.org

Le Musée Angladon
5 Rue Laboureur
84000 Avignon
+33 4 90 82 29 03
angladon.com

Le Musee Calvet
65 Rue Joseph Vernet
84000 Avignon
+33 4 90 86 33 84
musee-calvet.org

Le Musée Lapidaire
27 Rue de la République
84000 Avignon
+33 4 90 85 75 38
musee-lapidaire.org

Le Musée Louis Vouland
17 Rue Victor Hugo
84000 Avignon
+33 4 90 86 03 79
vouland.com

Le Musée du Petit Palais
Place du Palais des Papes
84000 Avignon
+33 4 90 86 44 58
petit-palais.org

Notre Dame des Doms
 and Le Jardin du rocher
 des Doms
Place du Palais des Papes
84000 Avignon

ANTIQUES

Colette Créange
18 Rue Joseph Vernet
84000 Avignon
+33 4 90 86 16 00

Gérard Guerre
Hôtel des Laurens
1 Plan de Lunel
84000 Avignon
+33 4 90 86 42 67

Hervé Beaume
19 Rue de la Petite Fusterie
84000 Avignon
+33 4 90 86 37 66
herve-baume.com

Ludovic Ramadier
3 Rue de la Grande Fusterie
84000 Avignon
+33 4 90 27 16 01

Martial Hanoun
14 Rue Carreterie
84000 Avignon
+33 4 90 82 00 46

Yannerick Serignan
8 Rue de la Petite Fusterie
84000 Avignon
+33 4 90 85 36 04
antiquite-serignan.com

HOMEWARES & GIFTS

La Boutique Desideco
17 Rue de la Petite Fusterie
84000 Avignon
+33 4 90 85 90 32

Cires et Senteurs
9 Place Saint Didier
84000 Avignon
+33 4 90 16 05 48
cires-et-senteurs.fr

Fanny et Baptistin
9 Rue Rouge
84000 Avignon
+33 4 32 74 27 89

HCG Créations
3 Rue Campane
84000 Avignon
+33 6 14 89 17 11

Hydropolis
(Bathroom accessories)
16 Rue de la Petite Fusterie
84000 Avignon
+33 4 90 27 38 19
hydropolis.fr

Au Jardin de Provence
2 Rue de la Petite Fusterie
84000 Avignon
+33 4 90 86 29 38

La Maison de Gegé
5 Place des Carmes
84000 Avignon
+33 6 16 86 66 28

La Maison du Fumeur
Cigars and pipes
16 Rue Saint-Agricol
84000 Avignon
+33 4 90 16 55 50

Mouvement
21 Place Crillon
84000 Avignon
+33 4 90 16 91 11
mouvement.com

Passé Présent
1 Place Saint Didier
84000 Avignon
+33 4 32 76 32 51

Senteurs du Soleil
12 Rue Carnot
84000 Avignon
+33 4 90 16 96 40

Souleiado
5 Rue Joseph Vernet
84000 Avignon
+33 4 90 86 47 67

Stylo Plume
45 Rue Joseph Vernet
84000 Avignon
+33 4 90 82 68 77

Terre è Provence
26 Rue de la République
84000 Avignon
+33 4 90 85 56 45

Vox Populi
32, Rue Vieux Sextier
84000 Avignon
+33 4 90 85 70 25
voxpopuli-deco.com

FASHION

Actuel B
11 Rue Joseph Vernet
84000 Avignon
+33 4 90 82 91 61

Cacharel
8 Rue Joseph Vernet
84000 Avignon
+ 33 4 90 86 19 19

Chapelier Mouret
(Hats)
20 Rue des Marchands
84000 Avignon
+33 4 90 85 39 38
chapelier.com

Coppelia
42 Rue Joseph Vernet
84000 Avignon
+33 4 90 82 10 40

Jean Rian
5 Rue Saint Agricol
84000 Avignon
+33 4 90 82 51 24

Laurence Molière Opticiens
(Glasses frames and sunglasses)
6 Rue Saint Agricol
84000 Avignon
+33 4 90 82 26 53

Parfumerie du Palais
(Perfumery)
1 Rue Saint Agricol
84000 Avignon
+33 4 90 85 52 63

Roma
(Lingerie and swimwear)
31 Rue Joseph Vernet
84000 Avignon
+33 4 90 27 93 63

So'oh
46 Rue Joseph Vernet
84000 Avignon
+33 4 90 85 74 66

FOOD, WINE & FLOWERS

Olivero
(Boulangerie)
60 Rue Carnot
84000 Avignon
+33 4 90 82 58 04

La Cave du Bouffart
5 Rue de la Monnaie
84000 Avignon
+33 4 90 82 24 30

Chocolaterie de Puyricard
33 Rue Joseph Vernet
84000 Avignon
+33 4 90 85 96 33
puyricard.fr

Comtesse du Barry
25 Rue Saint Agricol
84000 Avignon
+33 4 90 82 62 92
comtessedubarry.com

La Coupe d'Or
3 Place de Jérusalem
84000 Avignon
+33 4 90 82 18 31

Emotion et Tradition
(Florist)
39 Rue Joseph Vernet
84000 Avignon
+33 4 90 25 75 11

Le Fruitier de Saint Agricol
27 Rue Saint Agricol
84000 Avignon
+33 4 90 85 83 82
lefruitier.com

Jean-François Deldon
(Glacés and sorbets)
Artisan Glacier
35 Rue Saint Agricol
84000 Avignon
+33 4 90 85 59 41

Liquid
37 Rue de la Bonneterie
84000 Avignon
+33 4 90 85 19 89

Mallard
32 Rue des Marchands
84000 Avignon
+33 4 90 82 42 38

Oliviers & Co
19 Rue Saint Agricol
84000 Avignon
+33 4 90 86 18 41
oliviers-co.com

La Tropézienne
(Patisserie)
22 Rue Saint Agricol
84000 Avignon
+33 4 90 86 24 72

CINEMAS

Cinéma Utopia – La Manutention
4 Rue des Escaliers Sainte Anne
84000 Avignon
+33 4 90 82 65 36

Cinéma Utopia – République
5 Rue Figuière
84000 Avignon
+33 4 90 82 65 36
cinemas-utopia.org

HOTEL

La Mirande
4 Place de La Mirande
84000 Avignon
+33 4 90 14 20 20
la-mirande.fr

MARKETS

Marché paysan
(Food market)
Les Halles – undercover each
     morning from Tuesday to Sunday

Marché à la brocante
(Flea market)
Place Pie – Tuesday and
     Thursday morning
Rue Cabassole & Place des Carmes –
     Sunday morning.

Marché aux fleurs
(Flower market)
Place des Carmes – Saturday
     morning

Marché aux livres
(Book market)
Cours Jean Jaurès – the first
     Saturday of the month

VILLENEUVE-LÈS-AVIGNON

La Chartreuse Pontificale du
   Val-de-Bénédiction
Rue de la République
30400 Villeneuve-lès-Avignon
+33 4 90 15 24 24

La Collégiale Notre Dame
Town Centre
30400 Villeneuve-lès-Avignon

Le Fort Saint-André and
   L'Abbaye Saint-André
Mont Andaon
30400 Villeneuve-lès-Avignon

Le Musée Pierre de Luxembourg
3 Rue de la République
30400 Villeneuve-lès-Avignon
+33 4 90 27 49 66

Le Prieuré
(Hotel and restaurant)
7 Place du Chapitre
30400 Villeneuve-lès-Avignon
+ 33 4 90 15 90 15
leprieure.com

MARKETS

Marché paysan
(Food market)
Place Charles-David –
     Thursday morning

Marché à la Brocante
(Flea market)
Place Charles-David –
     Saturday morning

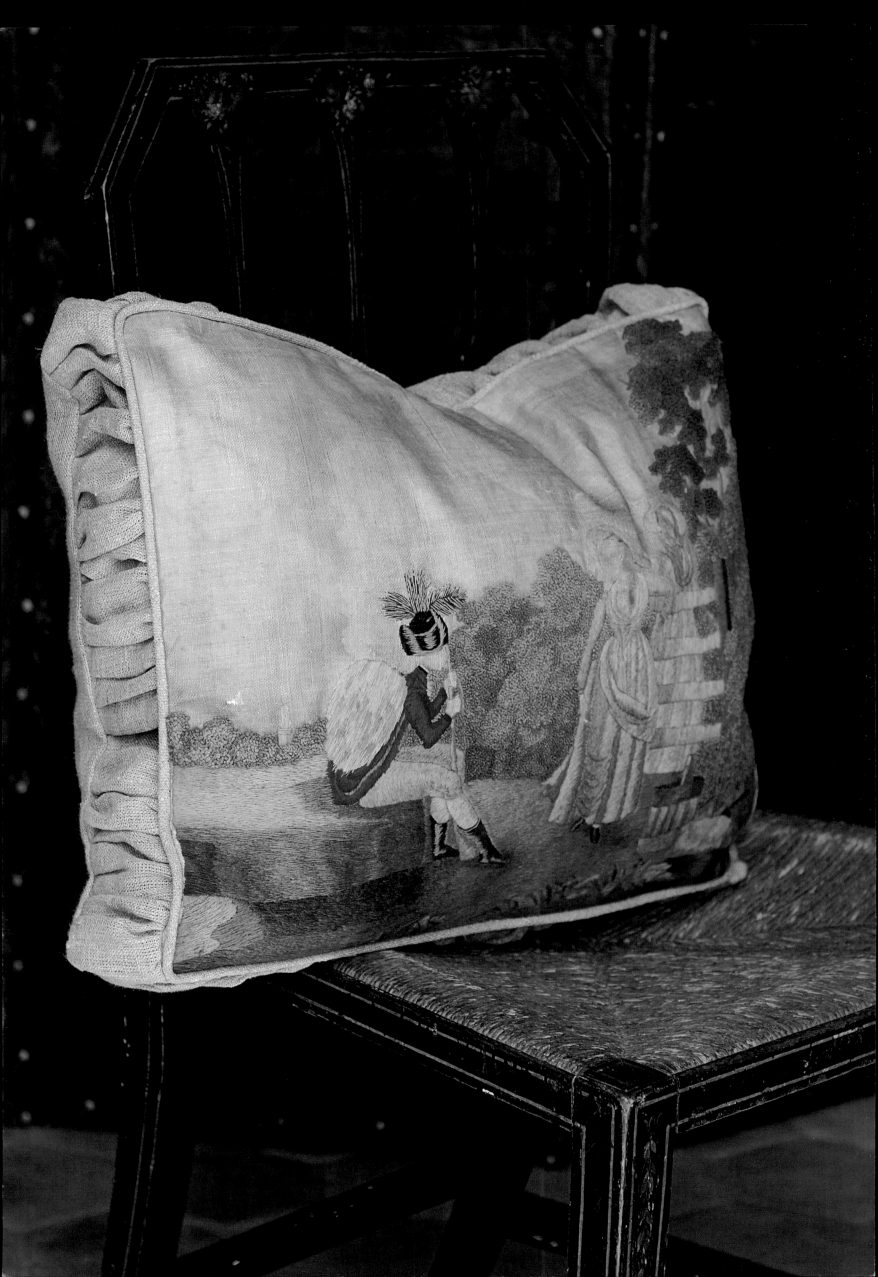

ACKNOWLEDGEMENTS

THE CONCEPTION AND PRODUCTION OF A BOOK are as much about the people behind the scenes as those on the title page. Without the creativity, boundless enthusiasm and wisdom of Julie Gibbs, the editorial strength and flair of Claire de Medici and the layout and design expertise of Adam Laszczuk, *French Essence* would not be; I cannot thank each of you enough.

The photography speaks for itself and I am forever grateful to Carla Coulson for not only her wonderful images but also the fun along the way. We spent many days styling at the *mas*, we explored Provence in search of beauty and we learned patience waiting for the perfect light. These behind-the-scenes days made *French Essence* a dream undertaking.

To Michel Semini: our garden is a joy and every day I am thankful for your vision.

Thank you to Jean-Benoît and Catherine Hugues, Gilles Culat, Emmanuelle and Sylvain Colombai, Cirque Stéphane Zavatta, L'Atelier Cézanne, La Mirande, La Maison du Village, Château d'Estoublon, Ciergerie des Prémontrés and Les Deux Garçons for giving so generously of their time.

To Lulu, Ahmed and Gérard: without you nothing would run smoothly.

To my friends who are such patient listeners and have helped me on countless occasions, thank you for your wise words and contributions: Guy, Charlie, Jack, Katy, Rachael, Polly and Cordelia; thank you for your gorgeous faces and endless smiles.

Lastly, none of this would have been possible without the love, encouragement and support of David, Emily, Venetia and Paddy.

LEFT - A favourite embroidered cushion.
FOLLOWING PAGE - Winter vines at Les Baux-de-Provence.

VIKING STUDIO
Published by the Penguin Group
Penguin Group (USA) Inc., 375 Hudson Street,
New York, New York 10014, U.S.A.
Penguin Group (Canada), 90 Eglinton Avenue East, Suite 700,
Toronto, Ontario, Canada M4P 2Y3
(a division of Pearson Penguin Canada Inc.)
Penguin Books Ltd, 80 Strand, London WC2R 0RL, England
Penguin Ireland, 25 St. Stephen's Green, Dublin 2, Ireland
(a division of Penguin Books Ltd)
Penguin Books Australia Ltd, 250 Camberwell Road, Camberwell,
Victoria 3124, Australia
(a division of Pearson Australia Group Pty Ltd)
Penguin Books India Pvt Ltd, 11 Community Centre, Panchsheel Park,
New Delhi – 110 017, India
Penguin Group (NZ), 67 Apollo Drive, Rosedale, North Shore 0632,
New Zealand (a division of Pearson New Zealand Ltd)
Penguin Books (South Africa) (Pty) Ltd, 24 Sturdee Avenue,
Rosebank, Johannesburg 2196, South Africa

Penguin Books Ltd, Registered Offices:
80 Strand, London WC2R 0RL, England

First American edition
Published in 2010 by Viking Studio,
a member of Penguin Group (USA) Inc.

1 3 5 7 9 10 8 6 4 2

Text copyright © Vicki Archer, 2009
Photographs copyright © Carla Coulson, 2009
All rights reserved

ISBN 978-0-670-02227-4

Design by Adam Laszczuk © Penguin Group (Australia)
Cover photograph by Carla Coulson
Colour reproduction by
Splitting Image Colour Studio Pty Ltd, Clayton, Victoria
Printed in China by 1010 Printing International Limited